Predator or Prince

How to Find the Man of Your Dreams, Not Your Nightmares

Dilys Sillah

Clink Street

London | New York

Published by Clink Street Publishing 2017

Copyright © 2017

First edition.

ISBN:
978-1-911525-55-4 - paperback
978-1-911525-56-1 - ebook

Foreword

One would imagine that a book entitled *Predator or Prince* would be an uncomplicated and straightforward read, especially since the title itself seems self-explanatory. Nothing could be further from the truth.

Find a comfortable space with no distractions and engulf yourself in a publication that is written with provocative, candid language sure to educate, inform, and equip its readers with knowledge. With the powerful wisdom Dilys Sillah shares in her book, readers will not only gain a deeper understanding of who they are, they will gain a deeper understanding of who they are in relationships.

As a woman who has overcome many debilitating situations such as addiction, childhood sexual abuse, mental illness, and other traumatic events, I began to research various sources to help me in my quest for understanding why I made some of the choices and decisions that led me to a place of brokenness, especially as it pertains to relationships.

Having written a best-selling memoir, *The Pink Elephant in the Middle of the GETTO,* I understand the amount of devotion it takes to write a book that will not only provide true examples and stories of its subject, but also provide preventative information as well as resources that will lead you to further healing long after you close the book. *Predator or Prince* has embodied this model and throughout this book Dilys Sillah effectively communicates her findings based on empirical research and statistical evidence.

Predator or Prince breaks down into easily understandable terms some of the most complicated patterns of relationships, such as the Father/Daughter Relationship, The Chameleon Syndrome, and Kissing the Frog and Finding the Prince. These chapters provide powerful insight as to why we as women make the choices we make and how we tend to change who we are to be in unhealthy relationships, more importantly, it tells us "why" we do this.

Again, I tell you: find a comfortable space in which to curl up with a cup of coffee and no distractions and become engulfed in the powerful presentation of erudition that will empower you and future generations to come.

Two thumbs up, five stars, and a smiley face for the woman who just made my relationship to my relationships make sense.

Be encouraged,

Trina "TiTi Ladette" Cleveland
Author of *The Pink Elephant in the Middle of the GETTO*

Chapter 1
So You're Ready To Date...

As women it seems no matter how old we are, what we look like or how we feel, self-assurance and confidence only seem to manifest when we've gone through a reflective MOT to bring us to a place of peace and love of self.

Acceptance of who we are, how we look, satisfaction in our chosen career paths and where we are in life generally, becomes a byproduct of coming to terms with the real us; the 'being comfortable in our own skin' kind of us.

The concept of cleansing the body, mind and soul puts us in a position of power, with the greatest asset being the power of choice; the power to exercise and express with confidence our balanced emotional needs.

When we are in this headspace, we are able to decide the rules of engagement in our interactions by working first on ourselves, before permitting anyone to come into our emotional space or 'mind field'.

From personal experience and observing the hundreds of women I've interacted with and taking note of the dynamics of those relationships, successful associations become quite elusive when we haven't gone through a cleansing of the heart process to self-evaluate our successes and failures.

We tend not to want to dwell on the failure part and just try and put it all behind us, because it may be too painful or require too much effort to work through the process that could take us to a place called 'Complete'; and to be honest, how many of us even know what that means?

The desire to be with someone becomes more of a deep need than a desire, and therein lies the key to limiting our options of how we operate with balance within the relationships we fall into.

In any relationship, and love relationships are no different, there's a level of authority we give a person over our being when we're not operating in a stable emotional or psychological capacity.

Wanting to be the other half in a relationship or a partnership is normal, but when it becomes all too consuming, when that need is dictated predominantly from an unhealthy place to complete and not complement us, the power of choice in who we associate with diminishes rapidly.

When we don't realise we're driven to be a part of a relationship that's masked to cover the wounds of either one or both individuals, the yardstick used to assess what is a balanced and well-rounded connection becomes impossible to measure, because the apparatus (i.e. our emotions) being used is flawed.

The measure of ability to determine soundness of judgement is there, provided everything is tweaked to function as intended.

All elements need to be aligned so the reading and accuracy of your assessment can reach a logical conclusion, which can only be done without false information that leads you to make decisions based on inaccuracies and illogical equations.

Fear of being alone can act as an enabler that prevents a person from ignoring the need to be practical and deliberate in assessing a potential partner's behaviours and the many other clues that we ignore.

Coming home to an empty bed and the lack of physical contact or adult conversation can be disheartening, lonely, frightening and isolating; it's an especially difficult state to be in if you were in a long term relationship and that relationship ended before you were ready to let it go, whether you walked out or they did.

Maybe you were bereaved, and that can be even harder to deal with for an array of reasons, ranging from the state of deep grief to regret, in wishing you'd done things differently, depending on what your particular story is.

A relationship between two people can be difficult enough to make work when you consider how complex we are as individuals. We all have our own identities and as unique as we are, no matter how connected we feel with another person, there's still the fact that you're two totally different people with differing views, differences in upbringing and life experiences to mention a few.

Time is needed to get to know each other and this can be both exciting and challenging, even when you claim to 'agree on everything': these observations are, of course, just a general take on how the dynamics of a regular relationship works for two regular people.

Step it up a notch and add children to the equation.

Children in the mix of a relationship, and the dynamics that this involves, becomes a very different ball game once you decide to date again; responsibly, that is!

When you've been in a relationship for a long time, you can sometimes lose a sense of self; be it with your self-confidence generally or trusting yourself to make decisions and plans that are right for you, that meet your particular needs.

Of course not all relationships are the same or end in the same way, but if you have been in a relationship where there has been a power imbalance of sorts, then you really need time to heal and find out who you are and what you want independently; ideally what you want and need is breathing and healing time.

It's helpful to explore the part you played in the relationship not working out, even where infidelity may have been involved, and that's not to say you should have given your partner more sex, nagged less or been a better cook!

No! No stereotypical, predictable blame-games here, just exploration and analysis of being better versions of ourselves and being sure of the world we want to see, create and experience for ourselves and our children particularly.

Nobody said it was ever easy to self-evaluate but where there's a will there's a way, and if your desire is to learn and grow, then you have to be willing to go where others fear to tread. You need to decide to be completely honest with yourself and it's going to take digging deep to do that, and maybe some external help and support to help facilitate it may be required.

Sometimes it's easier to do things in stages so we can better manage the change we're trying to implement.

Imagine you want to go for a swim and suspect the water is cold. You inch towards the pool with caution; dipping your toe in the water first, before your feet go in fully... then you climb in slowly and gently ease your body into the water. At times you pant and all the horrors of the cold water are etched on your face. Your arms are up in the air above your head as you continue to pant, then slowly but surely the water gets a little warmer with movement.

The arms come down and the muscles in your face start to relax. It's hard, but the longer you're in the water, the warmer it gets and the easier it becomes to swim.

If we can look within ourselves and self-evaluate with this attitude, eventually it will get easier and we'll seek to be in a continual state of self-assessment for the betterment of ourselves regardless of the temperature or depth of the water.

The process in our approach to get to know who we are will put us in a better place of knowing what we want in life and who we want to share it with. Uncertainty about who we are leads to confusion in various areas of our existence, and being clear on the kind of man we want to date isn't exempt from that confusion.

Throughout life we want things and then 'unwant' them because we have somehow grown older and wiser and see what we wanted was most certainly not what we needed, that we could live without the desired 'thing' once something better or more interesting came along.

We go back to that first dream that many little girls have of meeting Mr. Right and living happily ever after, only often life happens, and Mr. Right has been somewhat elusive so we settle for: Mr. Right Now, Mr. I Thought I Loved You, Mr. I Thought You Loved Me, Mr. I'll Make Do, even Mr. I'm Too Scared To Leave is hiding somewhere in that line-up.

The definition of what the perfect relationship is is ever up for debate and has been modernised through the ages. It's been adapted and repackaged to meet the sexual, emotional, financial, physical and even spiritual needs of those seeking to share themselves with another.

The real question is not what anyone else wants, but for you to know what you want... but what is really important is knowing what you most certainly DO NOT want in a relationship, and what you most certainly cannot afford to have in your home or around your children.

Chapter 2
Exploring Your Past...

'I cannot think of any need in childhood as strong as the need for a father's protection.' – Sigmund Freud

Isn't it funny how going back to childhood can mean different things to different people? Some of us can look back and be filled with great memories and varying degrees of nostalgia, with a deep yearning to go back in time to a place that was safe, happy and free.

A place without bills, mortgages and responsibilities, but with pimples, probably bad hair and a sense of uncertainty about ourselves that many of us are still trying to come to terms with today.

Family plays a massive part in forming childhood happiness or horrors, and it's very interesting how this contributes to determining the choices we make as adults in relationships because of it.

Some of these revelations seem so obvious, but it may or may not surprise you how many of us never sit down to analyse our childhood and try to investigate any possible correlations between our formative or younger years, and how they form or contribute to our personalities and how we act and think as adults.

As much as we don't like to go there – for good reason most probably – chances are the answers we are looking for to confirm our suspicions of who we are, are in there somewhere, or at least will act as a good starting point of exploration of who we are today.

When it comes to women or girls and the men we date, we've heard the phrase 'wanting a father-figure' many times.

I'm sure we all know the term is usually descriptive of a female that is partial to older men who normally remind them of the father they never knew or the father they did.

Consciously or subconsciously, women often use their father/daughter relationship as a yardstick for future romantic connections and I think the reason for this is very simple.

For these women, their fathers are the first male/female relationship they experience. Fathers are the ones to hold the most influence of what a man is or should be, as they stand as a representation of all men as far as the perception of a young girl child is concerned, so the father is the most impressionable relationship a girl will ever have with any other male.

The dynamics of how that relationship works becomes both the foundation and the template for future interactions, for the grown female child and her chosen mate.

I use the word 'impressionable' intentionally, as validation and acceptance is what all children need from a father; for the purpose of what we are trying to explore here, I will concentrate on the female child and her father in this instance.

Girls love their daddies. If 'Daddy' plays his role well by being the perfect prototype for future male relationships, then he would have done his job well.

The validation and sense of belonging and security a daughter feels in relation to her father, when she is told how much she is loved and smart and beautiful, is invaluable in building up the female child to be a woman that has self-confidence and is self-assured. This form of nurturing greatly minimises the need to be validated by any man in the future, as there are no major emotional voids that need to be filled.

Other factors may arise during the course of her life, but the validation of a father does reduce the need to look for a man to fill any holes in the heart; of course this validation may not totally eradicate the possibility of a woman or girl entering into a bad relationship, but the reasons for it may be attributed to other experiences on her life's journey.

Having a father that is present and involved physically, and is a positive character and influence, is the obvious ideal, but is there really such a thing as an absent father?

The relationship formed in the mind of a child whose father is not physically present can be just as powerful as one that is experienced in a physical relationship.

Never underestimate the power and strength of emotions the 'present absent' father can conjure in the daughter who doesn't know him in real life.

Reality is as real as we want it to be. The only evidence of reality in the mind of a girl whose father hasn't been around is what she says to herself is evidence.

The idea that her father is the most wonderful man on earth, and is only absent for whatever reason, allows the child to put in the necessary coping mechanisms and make the needed excuses to make the rejection not feel like rejection, but rather there being perfectly plausible reasons as to why her father doesn't come and claim her.

The child that holds anger and resentment for being deprived of a relationship with their father may exhibit the total opposite in behaviour in terms of the picture she paints in her mind.

Vowing never to let any man mess them about and be dependent on them. Never allowing themselves to be hurt or to be weak, but rather being the one to display power, and steely determination to be strong and not be vulnerable or show signs of weakness, especially when it comes to matters of the heart.

In all of this, there is the mother.

The mother is a crucial part to this picture and how she is 'permitted' to function in the dynamics of the home also forms an integral part of the blueprint for the male/female relationship for that child.

The female child will grow, understanding her position in the home and the role she is to play within it, based largely on what she has witnessed growing up.

As little girls love their daddies, so also do little girls want to be 'just like mummy'. Those of you who answer to that name are more than likely already aware that gives you immediate idol status in the eyes of the little one who is probably already using your lipstick, trying on your heels and wearing your jewelry.

It's really interesting that even when we are the dominant parties in a relationship in an unhealthy way, the dynamics of this type of union also has an effect on how children emulate or shy away from the behaviours they've been exposed to.

There is still an expectation from the girl child of her father to be a father. There is never any excuse or reason that is satisfying to a child for a father not to be the protector, the nurturer, the hero and to just be there to give love and reassurance as and when required.

It is very important, even at this stage, that we are very clear that as we are exploring the dynamics of our foundational years, that we stop… and pause for a moment… and think what our children are witnessing in our own homes at this precise moment, and the pictures we are painting for them and the experiences we are giving them.

What you tolerate, voluntarily or involuntarily, is forming the reality for her home life and who she will invite into it in years to come.

The effects of negative and damaging experiences in the home life of children both male and female manifest differently, but are damaging with lasting effects nonetheless.

Each sex manifests the effects of a negative home life differently and yet sometimes quite similarly.

For example, girls may be eager to start a family of their own by wanting to settle down early. This usually happens to try and create a new world and existence for themselves in order to put in place all the things they never had.

The idea of having a baby and having 'someone to love me' is a very common mindset of girls who have been neglected or rejected by those that should have loved and cared for them. The thought of being able to establish the perfect home often turns out to be the opposite that is achieved, primarily because the emotional authority and power which one requires to be able to execute such a plan needs soul searching, healing and a wholeness to make it possible. These answers, I hope, we can explore together and find some of them here.

Male children don't often go off to get married and try and procreate to forget their traumatic upbringing. Behavioural problems, issues with anger, drug and alcohol experimentation are some of the outlets that boys (and girls too but often in conjunction with the above) may choose to use to deal with the issues that have gone on in their lives.

As I mentioned, girls use these same methods too, but somehow where their male counterparts may be able to be notorious for their antics and gain a form of respect in their connections, somehow girls don't seem to quite have the same 'results' in being able to exert their behaviours in a way that serves them in their romantic connections.

Chapter 3
Your First Love...

The one thing we never forget is our first love.

The first time you fall in love is forever etched in your mind and forever in your heart. The things he said, the things you did together, the plans you made. The first time of everything that you ever did including 'that thing' isn't something that is ever forgotten.

You look at that relationship and look at what was beautiful or not so beautiful about it, and if it falls within the latter category then we sometimes have a tendency to rewrite history to make it that little more special or more than likely, that little more bearable.

I guess the height of joy or the depth of pain is determined by where you are on your journey and subsequent relationship success, and the lessons you have learnt from your first major emotional encounter.

The positioning of that first love in our memory bank either earns him a seat on a pedestal or his head as a footstool; either way, our second prototype holds another important position in our emotional hall of fame.

When a girl or woman falls in love for the first time, it usually is with all that she has; she holds nothing back. Her love is given freely and is accepting of her mate, uncomplicated and above all 'believing and trusting'. It's in the believing and trusting that forms the very foundation for the maximum amount of destruction and damage to be experienced, when that belief and trust is displaced or betrayed.

It's always interesting how the older, wiser and more experienced can usually tell a mile off that the new beau or first love in our life is not the one.

They have an eye to know instinctively that the young man is not who he portrays himself to be but love is blind, they say, and we fail not only to spot the signs, but to listen to those who have.

With all things in life, experience is supposed to teach us how best to deal with situations in whatever areas of our lives in a forward-thinking, proactive way, but is seems experience isn't applied as well as it can be when it involves matters of the heart.

The heart is a funny old thing, and seems to have an emotional mind of its own; once it disconnects from the head, you might find you emotionally flatline and lose the very essence for which your heart was intended.

The heart and head work best in partnership, and are what we really should refer to as a match made in heaven.

Falling in love for the first time, for many of us, is an experience that takes place in our younger years, such as our teens; a time already fraught with emotional ups and downs due to the very nature of adolescence.

We aren't really emotionally equipped to understand exactly what is going on with our bodies; the awkwardness of being halfway between an adult and a child can be very confusing and can make many young people feel they are being pulled emotionally from pillar to post.

With an already overwhelming amount of activity going on in the adolescent mind and body, a failed relationship where the subject has been in love makes things that little more emotionally and mentally explosive.

We the all-knowing adults tend to scoff at 'young love' and have an air of flippancy when having to listen to the hurt and pain that is being witnessed, but it is no laughing matter if you can appreciate the long term effects that unresolved emotional matters of the heart have on the decisions that are made for relationships following that experience.

I've always had a fascination with relationships and why some fail and others don't, so I guess it's not too surprising that no matter what career paths I have taken, I've always had some connection or hand in being involved through counselling or coaching people in this area.

One thing that totally baffled me in the past but only made sense when I 'grew up' was something I found quite bizarre at the time.

Many years ago I dated a young man who was about 23 at the time.

I recall very early on when we first starting dating, we were sitting down having a chat and got onto the subject of relationships.

I noticed he had a chain around his neck, which I didn't think much of as it looked dingy and discoloured and just seemed a bit out of place for some reason.

Thinking it was a total change of subject on my part, I asked where he had gotten the chain from.

He began to tell me a very distressing story of how he had been in love and had had his heart broken by the person who had given the chain to him.

I naturally felt sorry for him because he was visibly getting quite distraught. By this time, he was telling me how this girlfriend of his had lied to him, left him and broken his heart. He had kept the chain around his neck as a reminder of their relationship and how much she had meant to him.

I assumed that this horrid breakup had been quite recent and obviously messy. Maybe she had cheated on him or left him for his best friend or something, so I asked when they'd dated, and this is when my jaw dropped: he told me that he was TWELVE YEARS OLD when he had 'dated' this girl who broke his heart! T.W.E.L.V.E.!

I could not believe it. I could not believe that at twelve he had been so in love, and practically eleven years later was recalling the effects of that break up to the point of crying uncontrollably at the hurt he had experienced as if it were yesterday.

When I got over the shock, (and I tried desperately not to look it) I coaxed him to take the chain off and try to put it all behind him and move on, and he did.

As inexperienced as I was then, I knew that this reaction to me wasn't 'normal' and definitely felt uncomfortable.

To be honest I wasn't in love but did care about him so I carried on getting to know him, knowing my feelings were unlikely to progress beyond fondness.

I realised as time went on that he was quite besotted with me but at the time that wasn't cause for concern to me.

I'd had the pleasure of meeting his parents and they were really lovely… then there were his sisters, who bar one were just rude and horrid.

After meeting them and their constant jibes and attitude, I didn't think there was enough there for me to hang around, so I decided to end the relationship.

What had brought it on was a very awkward dinner I had attended with him and his family. As I recall, his sisters were particularly nasty and I had to order a cab and leave due to their bullying antics.

He was the only boy of the family and I think the thought of some girl coming in and taking their brother away was a bit too much for them to bear, so I bore the brunt of their snide comments at dinner for longer than I thought was acceptable, but what I really found unacceptable was my date's complete inability to defend me from the pack of wolves I was forced to eat with.

So the next time he came to see me after the incident with his sisters, I remember we were in his car outside my parents' house. I said that I thought it would be better to be friends as we didn't seem to have too much in common and let him know that I also didn't want to put him in a position where he felt he had to choose between me and his family because I could see how close they were.

I first saw the tears, then he immediately started to hit his fists on the steering wheel and started begging me not to leave him; I admit I was scared and totally taken aback.

He was quite a gentle character and this wasn't the kind of reaction I'd expected. I knew he'd be disappointed but not to the point of displaying such an outburst, in total contrast to the person I thought he was.

I felt I had to pretend my desire to end the relationship was a mistake on my part in order to feel I could control the situation, so that's what I did. He did eventually calm down and stopped crying and banging the steering wheel.

I went home and he drove off and I thought that was that.

So come morning, I rang him to find out how he was. He said something that made me ask what time he had returned home.

I was shocked when he told me he had never arrived home; he had spent the night in his car parked opposite my house because he wanted to be close to me.

That revelation completely unnerved me and I knew I had to think smart if I wanted to get out of the relationship with as little drama and as few outbursts as possible.

Now I'm not advocating anyone tries this but in my nineteen-year-old head, this was the best I could come up with:

I told my boyfriend that I wanted to marry him and have his children… immediately. I said if he loved me that much he would marry me. I didn't think most 23-year-old guys would swap their freedom to walk down the aisle so quickly, so I hedged my bets on him running a merry mile; I was right!

He was prepared for us to have a child but not get married. I told him that in the family I came from, my parents would disown me so he would have to marry me. As neither of us were willing to compromise, we agreed to part company as friends because we both wanted different things.

There were a lot of tears, mostly his (mine were of relief), but I had managed to extricate myself from him in a way that he didn't feel abandoned by me and I felt safe.

The prospect of him being outside my home whilst I was sleeping just gave me the creeps.

We went our separate ways and we occasionally kept in touch.

A few months later, I learnt he died whilst on a trip with his workmates in France; I was so sad to hear the news.

I had been abroad when I received the phone call some time after his death, so wasn't able to attend the funeral; I later heard his sisters had told all his friends I hadn't attended his send off because I couldn't be bothered. It's something that has hurt me deeply but did confirm to me why even those actions from his sisters told me I had absolutely made the right decision to leave; bullying and intimidation from anyone isn't acceptable.

So why am I sharing this memory with you?

Well, it goes to show how deeply negative experiences in love can seriously affect and shape how we act and feel.

Though the example I've given is about how a negative experience affected a young man, the fact is that young man was manifesting the damage of his experience in his relationship with me, and this is where I make the correlation.

I could have very easily been a victim of a very unhealthy union because his childhood trauma hadn't been dealt with.

I cannot categorically say what the future would have held for us if I had decided to hang around, but what I do know from the little I saw was that he bore the hallmarks of some of the traits that abusive men often exhibit.

His desire to avoid a repeat of his experience as a boy appeared to have him wanting to behave in a way that wouldn't leave him feeling vulnerable or abandoned again.

When people feel that their greatest fear is about to come back and claim them, they go into survival mode, and I think this is what he started to exhibit in the car that night.

That survival mode, in my experience and observations, usually means methods need to be applied in the relationship to ensure that you stay, no matter what and at any cost. Emotional, domestic and psychological abuse are usually the three courses served in these circumstances, the innate need to control.

I have spoken to quite a few men about the first time they fell in love and one common trend I noticed was that where their relationships hadn't ended on their terms, and they were left heartbroken, they subsequently had a very nonchalant attitude towards relationships and very rarely became deeply emotionally involved with the women or girls they dated.

It's interesting how the reactions for both boys and girls, men and women are so different in how they manifest their relationship let-downs and how they deal with rejection.

It is every bit normal to want to be loved and validated by the relationships we are welcomed or born into, so the end of a first-love relationship that has been intense and ends on bad terms can cause emotional or psychological trauma.

The effects can take a young person through a whole spectrum of feelings likened to one who has been bereaved.

Anger, frustration, disbelief, disappointment, loneliness, depression, a feeling of very low self-worth and rejection, are some of what can be experienced to varying degrees following the severing of those love ties.

It is highly unlikely that teenagers and young adults that go through this experience will be offered counselling and support in a structured and professional capacity, to rebalance and restore their mental and emotional health. In essence they are left to their own devices to figure out how they get over the damage that was caused and are expected to 'grow up' and just get on with it… after all, what do they know about real love?

Once the damage has indeed been done, this second foundation of how the dynamics of the way relationships work is set.

For girls who have not had those formative years validated by the father, this can mean the desire to want to be loved and accepted intensifies even more when entering into subsequent relationships after the first failed love. The need to protect one's heart is done somewhat back-to-front by wanting to adapt oneself to fit into the other person's definition of being loveable, thinking that by remodeling, adapting and suppressing who they are, they are now somehow easier to love and therefore less likely to be rejected and left by their new mate.

As we keep giving concessions to new partners, what we invariably end up doing is giving ourselves away for free, having removed all value from ourselves.

Chapter 4
The Chameleon Syndrome...

A chameleon is described as being a small, slow-moving Old World lizard with a prehensile tail, long extensible tongue, protruding eyes that rotate independently, and *a highly developed ability to change colour...*

Not a particularly pretty picture, but one that is very apt and totally fit for purpose in determining why this comparison of ourselves and this wonderful creature is being made.

Chameleons have several layers of specialised cells called chromatophores. These cells are responsible for the chameleon's changing colour. For example, the chameleon will change its colour to regulate its body heat as it's the only way it can maintain a favourable body temperature.

Here is another example: the female changes colour when it's ready to mate, whilst the male will go dark when they are in an aggressive mood. Of course there is so much more to find out about this creature but there is enough information to understand the nature of the chameleon, and one of its main characteristics is its ability to change colour dependent on its mood, its needs and its intentions.

Our need for acceptance can sometimes drive us to pretend extensively in situations where we may be uncomfortable being our true selves or where we feel we need to protect ourselves. This may be the case when we are nervous, uncomfortable, afraid or just not willing to be laid bare for a whole range of reasons. We fear being transparent because being vulnerable is not something many of us are comfortable with because we fear the unknown. We don't want to take the chance of being transparent unless we are guaranteed that our vulnerability and emotional exposure will not be used against us.

The need for acceptance can make us behave in ways that don't necessarily come naturally to us. Not in a way that makes a person hypocritical in the typical sense of the word, but in a way that is dictated by the relationships we are in and our responding to both the verbal and nonverbal demands of our partner, and how we respond to those demands to ensure we stay relevant to them.

Remember in the description of the characteristics of the chameleon we learnt that it has a *'highly developed ability to change colour'*. Let's substitute the word *'colour'* for the word *'character'*.

There are many facets to us as females. There are also varying intricate layers like the chameleon that we get to discover in more and more detail as we get older, layers that we sometimes do not even know we have.

The different experiences we go through, the things we are exposed to, the situations we find ourselves in and our interactions with others, both positive and negative, determine the varying shades of colour that invariably shape and design us.

Much of what we do before we find ourselves is driven to be more accepted or liked, and we often try to act in a way that we think will make people more accepting of us. We hide essentially what is our true self, so we don't stand out too much for all the 'wrong' reasons. The desire to be part of the pack or be invited into the pack directs us to act in this way.

There are many reasons for this ranging from culture to religious beliefs and societal stereotypes to name a few, and many other contributory factors.

Within each of these areas, we're expected to perform the function that others place on us. Our fear of not being accepted has us acting out the roles that are imposed on us consciously or subconsciously, with little regard for how it makes us feel until the cost of these impositions puts us in the red, having made us overdrawn from our emotional bank accounts.

When in relationships, is where our colours quickly change, but unlike the chameleon, the colour change is not for our benefit. It's not to regulate our 'heat' or to signal our intentions, but rather to accommodate what is normally emotional, physical, sexual or psychological inappropriate behaviour of our mate.

We make excuses and we reason that the hurt or pain we are being subjected to is either something we have brought upon ourselves or somehow responsible for putting right.

Even in the simplest of circumstances our colour changes as soon as we sense that our mate is unhappy. We begin to morph into a chameleon of sorts by sacrificing our need to be comforted and heard; disallowing our mate to take rightful responsibility in acknowledging their wrongdoing or recognise they have caused pain and for them to take ownership for it and responsibility for putting it right.

Even when not at fault, we often flick on the 'understanding switch'. We begin to reason out the behaviour of our mate by ignoring what we typically should communicate but shy away from, in order to avoid confrontation and avoid responses such as the silent treatment. We accommodate the attitude and ride the storm and wait patiently for it to pass so we can carry on as 'normal'.

We fear to run the risk of frightening off our partner by being honest about how we really feel, so invariably when there is a disagreement, we recoil and let the situation ride its course until there is what seemingly appears to be harmony restored.

This is of course until the next time there is a disagreement or you are unhappy and the cycle is repeated.

The more this pattern is repeated, the more this particular dynamic of the relationship of keeping silent to hide your needs is reinforced and established. That is: neither you nor your feelings are as important as your mate's. That your needs are secondary and that you are solely responsible for the 'relationship thermometer' in your union.

This gives rise to subservience in the makeup of the relationship and becomes a scale of power, tipping heavily against the female.

As we continue to show various shades of the different types of our colour, we begin to see them all blend into one where we cease to be able to differentiate between one colour and the next.

The continual process of convincing ourselves over time that either we or our needs don't matter or are secondary, takes us one step away from our true selves and one step closer to the type of male that seeks out a person who has now become colourblind and emotionally dependent or wanting.

It is completely possible that someone can go through this process and be totally unaware that they are denying their own needs, usually for a partner who is largely undeserving.

It is far more beneficial, like the chameleon, to be in control of their colour change. To understand its own needs and through second nature instinct, making independent decisions and adequate provision to ensure those needs are met. The meeting of those needs is not interdependent on the contribution of the mate, and neither is the solution to the meeting of those needs provided by the mate.

Every requirement to identify, process and seek a solution is there, in its totality to meet all needs, requiring no substantial input if any, to meet the needs of the female if that need is emotional. The female can control all colours required for the purpose for which she needs to adapt.

Our colour change frequently translates to and indicates that we are unclear on who we are because we have trained or convinced ourselves that we don't matter enough to establish our identity before entering into a relationship.

The need for acceptance and the fear of being alone and trying to avoid that overrides any need for self-validation, self-confidence, and self-assurance.

Because we fail to establish who we are, we essentially parade a number of different shades, likened to a colour chart when choosing colours to paint a room; we invariably present our mate or potential mate to make the choice by picking a colour.

Once the colour has been chosen, we act out the chosen shade to match and benefit the other person by adopting a persona that is really an alien part of us – if it wasn't, there would be no colour chart on offer…

What would be helpful to realise is that rejection is a part of life and a necessary evil we have to live with throughout our stay on Earth.

Like many things that appear to be negative on the surface, it can indeed be a blessing in disguise. The issue is not the rejection per se, but our definition of what rejection is, our first experience of it, how it was dealt with and the likelihood of it being repeated or relived in the same capacity; this is why confidence in self, that strong foundation of self-belief can be so powerful and is so important. Why? Because we will be able to separate our experience from who we are. In other words, we are not our rejection, we are not our trauma, we are not our rape, we are not our abuse, we are not our domestic violence.

It's very sad when the effects of a break up of a relationship have such devastating consequences on our emotional and mental selves that some of us feel that life isn't worth living. These feelings can send us into the depths of depression and despair, as if there is nothing worth living for if the other person who has rejected us is no longer a part of our world; the truth is, there is always something better around the corner.

If the person who has rejected you has made you feel worthless in the process or during the course of your relationship, it should not be too difficult to fathom another human being that is even slightly above the standard that has previously been accepted by you.

Because our self-worth is cleverly and systematically chipped away, it clouds our ability to judge others and ourselves objectively, putting aside feelings and to be factual, basing our assertions on evidence, as opposed to deep rooted emotions that drive our assessments, which are steeped in flawed foundations.

If we are able to understand the core of our being and who we are, rejection will be embraced as part of a journey and not seen or interpreted as a final destination. We will dwell there for a little while, and when we have mustered enough strength, assessed and analysed what went wrong and the lessons learnt, we will gather ourselves and move on to the next destination with the knowledge we have acquired from the experience.

We will move on a little wiser with a new sense of purpose, understanding and determination; umbrella in case it rains, hiking boots for any mountains we may encounter and a life jacket for any rivers with deep unknown currents that may not be visible to the naked eye.

Whatever the weather, we'll be OK to 'weather the storm', to dance in the rain or bask in the sunshine; whatever the weather, we will be OK.

Chapter 5
Kissing the Frogs,
Finding the Prince...

How many fairytales did we read as young girls growing up, where the princess had to kiss a frog for him to turn into the handsome prince he once was and was always supposed to be?

We already know how impressionable young girls can be and society shapes little girls from a very early age into what they should become after telling them who they are.

A lot of this is done so unconsciously, and probably unintentionally, that it's hard to see the possible harmful underlying messages in these stories.

Children are encouraged to let their imagination run wild because it's a positive thing to stimulate the mind of a child, enabling their creativity and enhance their own imaginative capabilities and writing skills. It appears no real boundaries are set for the projection of possible limiting beliefs challenged, for the damage they may cause.

I want to explore a well-known fairytale so we can take a look at this picture and analyse the subliminal message here:

The Princess and the Frog:

Apparently (I haven't been able to prove this) there was a

beautiful princess that had to kiss a frog to break a terrible spell that had been placed on him by a wicked witch.

The princess was his only chance to break free and be the lovely handsome prince he really was…

The princess was lonely and was looking for someone to keep her company.

Let's consider this scenario of The Princess And The Frog.

My understanding of this story tells us that the frog is only a frog due to circumstances but underneath it all, he's really a handsome prince just waiting for the right woman to look beyond his flaws, plant him a kiss on the lips and voila! A fine young gentleman will emerge with no sign of his 'froggy' past.

Some women and girls have a tendency to want to 'fix' the boys and men they date or end up marrying.

It is not unusual for women to feel that they have the power or ability to turn another human being to fit into who they want them to be; truth is, we rarely succeed in doing so.

The story of The Princess And The Frog had another interesting element to it: The princess lost her ball(s) and the frog said he could retrieve it for her, at a small cost of course – he had to live with her and be her companion if he succeeded.

When the princess was given her ball she forgot about her promise and but was swiftly reminded by the King that she had to keep her word… Interesting… not much has changed in the real world, where women are bound by the vows they take at all costs, no matter what.

In real life, some of us encounter frogs, and will unwittingly kiss these frogs only to find that they remain a frog. No 'voila' moment, no fanfare of seeing their frog morph into a handsome prince. No! The frog remains, only his croak has become louder.

The frog is a deceiver who is relying on history and past glory to lure the unsuspecting female into buying into his flaws, shortcomings, deception and unsubstantiated silent promises of his ability to change.

The reality is that we overlook what we can clearly see, denying the evidence of what we witness just to fuel a dream we read in a story book at the age of five.

They say love is blind but it isn't; it chooses not to see and there is a very clear distinction between the two.

If a man presents himself in one way, then he is that way. It is in every females best interest not to try to understand it, interpret it or make excuses for it. It's only your responsibility to recognise it, and if you must offer kisses, only offer kisses with your eyes wide open.

Because of our dreams of magic and fairytale endings, relationships are entered into with a displaced hope that things will change because the power to effect change has been placed in our 'kiss'.

We put ourselves in the position of some sort of Messiah to alter the course of a relationship because we have assumed a position only the man in question can take, and that is to be wholly in charge of himself and take the responsibility to change as his priority.

This ability to change is something that should remain squarely on his shoulders and not on your emotions or your conscience, or indeed in your 'kiss'.

If your love interest is so far removed from what you want and what you should expect from a relationship, such as the very basics being love, respect, appreciation, loyalty etc., then you need to think very seriously about why you would be willing to compromise, and believe you have the power to change another person when the real work should be performed on yourself.

Am I saying that you don't give people a chance or be supportive or caring to someone in need? Of course not, but in the context of what we are exploring here, the answer will need to be answered with a question:

Would you be happy, content and satisfied and OK with the fact that your choice of man remained a frog? Because if not, ask yourself why you did the honours of offering a kiss to change the man if you really didn't mind the state he was in when you met him? Why is it necessary to enter into a relationship to give that support? Would it not serve you better to see those changes taking place before adding your emotional self as part of those dynamics?

The ideal is to be in a place of no compromise under any circumstances, if the compromise is around your values, your safety, your emotional stability and whatever else is important to you.

We need to explore and identify the things that set us back and cause us to be derailed in life.

We have got to be selfish when it comes to our peace of mind and our emotional, mental and physical health.

The old saying of charity beginning at home is so true, and even more so in what we are exploring.

You need to look within and work on yourself before you can be the emotional fountain you want your mate to draw from if you don't want to run dry.

You can't give what you don't have, and it is impossible – and there are no exceptions here to have a healthy and well balanced relationship if you're emotionally unstable, needy or have unresolved issues from your past.

Acting as the rescuer in any relationship presents an unwritten contract for your mate not to have to take responsibility in the relationship and sometimes in many other areas too.

If you're dating a man, let him be a man: whole, emotionally available, respectful and possessing all the traits you can expect of a 'good man'. If you find that you can't identify any of these in the man or men you've dated, then I would suggest you go back to the beginning of this book and ponder a little longer on what may be the cause and reason for that.

If you have children, begin to think of the picture you're painting for them.

You cannot afford to take your kids on a discovery journey with you when it comes to relationships – only you should walk the green mile of a relationship.

True power really lies with us being able to change ourselves, our view of the world and the part we play in it.

Chapter 6
Meet the Kids...

'Hi kids! Meet your Uncle Tom'... or is that Uncle Dick or Uncle Harry?

As much as we may assume that children like to do what they want, when they want and how they want, they often desire the contrary because children not only like order, they thrive on it.

Order in the home and clear boundaries shows there is a level of care, love and concern for their welfare and allows them to be accountable for their actions and the values that you are raising them with. The order in the home also allows the parent to gauge what has been instilled in them and allows the framework that has been set to include how behaviours that are contrary to the standards in the home are to be identified and addressed.

In a home where there is neither consistency, set boundaries nor order, it may be difficult for children to recognise or know what standard of behaviour to adhere to, because the messages are confusing and it will be unclear when those lines are being crossed or the consequences, if any, for crossing them.

When a mother brings a new mate home who obviously is not the father of her children, that new mate is met with an element of automatic suspicion, caution or dislike, simply because he is not their father.

The onus lies with the mother to ease the children into a place where they feel they are able to get to know the new partner in order to make a determination for themselves, whether they like or want him to be a part of their home or indeed a part of their mother's life.

Their choice should be without pressure and their opinion should be considered for whatever that opinion is. Even if seemingly unfounded, it's indicative of something that requires attention and at the very least consideration.

Children can sometimes be far more discerning than adults, with the ability to sense and see beyond what grown ups may miss and what a person might hide.

It is important that when a new man is being introduced into the home, time is spent getting to know the person before you introduce them to your kids.

Of course you can never know a person 100%, but time is always a great enabler in getting to know a person to a degree; that is why it's important that if you haven't gotten to know the very basics of your new mate, that you do so independently of your children.

There is no reason more important than your children when considering whether to introduce a new partner or move a new man into the home hastily, as it is not just you that will feel the effects or face the consequences of a break up if and when it happens, and there are far more serious things that could happen besides this.

The introduction of new boyfriends into the home indiscriminately can be a cause of great instability for your children and is the beginning of seeds of negative ideas of commitment, relationships and love to impressionable children, regardless of their age.

It is our duty as mothers to protect our children emotionally as well as physically, and the exposure to every partner that you date will cause your children to be suspicious and unwilling to give emotionally.

Instability in the home pushes children to seek stability elsewhere, and the 'elsewheres' are seldom good substitutes of what should have been part of the fabric of their home life.

With constant men coming in and out of the home, the other message is that relationships are not meant to last and aren't consistent. To young minds, these observations and conclusions aren't positive relationship images.

The attachment and connection a child experiences with someone they feel is a constant in their life turns to a feeling of abandonment when that person leaves. They are seldom privy to the reasons for the relationship breakdown so are unable to process the reasons why that person has left and is no longer a part of their lives. They are not a part of the process of the relationship breakdown in terms of reasons, so there is no preparation for when the relationship ends. It's only when the person is no longer there that they're forced to deal with the reality of the breakup and left wondering what went wrong.

Very rarely are children given a balanced account of a relationship breakup. Aside from having to deal with the end of the union between their mother and her partner, the child is left having to deal with the offloading of the mother's emotional burdens in the form of anger, pain, disappointment and whatever else she's feeling.

It's a lot for children to have to deal with.

I've said before how children love with everything they have and to have to deal with the rejection of that love – intentional or not – acts as a negative picture of how this whole love thing works.

Of course nobody can predict the future; things happen. Partners leave, partners die, people drift apart, but this isn't the issue if the manner in which these things are handled and communicated is one that makes sense to a child.

It is uncommon for children to be given any emotional support in these circumstances either, therefore this is another scenario where they are left to navigate their emotional minefield to rebalance themselves following a loss of sorts or a severance of a relationship.

What would be the real reason any woman would feel the need to have every partner she dates be part of her family makeup or children's lives? Could it be that there is a deep emotional void or insecurities within her that seemingly are less 'visible' once in a relationship? Is it a fear of being alone? A sense of only feeling worthy if they are in relationship, regardless of who it's with or if they are being treated right?

Whatever the reason, those problems can only be resolved by the one person who has a choice in this scenario and that is you – the mother, the person who is ultimately responsible and accountable for herself and the welfare of her children.

The abuser and the sexual predator can sense like a tracking dog a woman who has these emotional needs within a very short space of time; it is for these reasons that he is willing to move into your home or make official his relationship with you as quickly as possible before you spot the signs.

The abuser doesn't often have the ability to mask who he is indefinitely, he really doesn't, so time is of the essence to him.

You need to make time work for you by biding yours in order to evaluate who your man is and how he behaves around different people and in different circumstances. The mask of a predator always needs adjusting and repositioning because knowledge and time is his number one enemy.

There are always signs, but it's knowing what to look out for; however the greatest sign of all being who you are and what you project at the point of entering into the relationship.

The more self-assured, secure, comfortable in your own skin, in love with yourself, at peace with your past and present, accepting of your faults… the more you are all these things, the less likely and the less attractive you are to the abuser and the predator.

They can only survive on your insecurity, naivety, fear, self-hate, lack of love for self and an innate need to be loved. Like bacteria, they need a host – the predator cannot survive otherwise.

You will more often than not attract who you are; if you can figure out who you are, then you can attract who you want and repel who you don't; this is why the work has to start from within.

Abusive men are weak. They are frightened boys in men's bodies. They are insecure. They are scared. They feel worthless. They have no real power.

If we really understood how unworthy they are of our love and more so our fear, we would present the strength we are capable of possessing. It is my desire that we find the strength within us to overcome the things in life that have kept us bound, because we can do it.

Predator or Prince

Chapter 7
Instincts – Your Child Has
Them Too...

Depending on your culture, traditions and your upbringing, this will determine how loud a voice your child has.

No race has every single person within it exactly the same but for the purpose of demonstration, a generalisation of certain groups will explain the point:

Being of African origin, from the Western part of Africa – Ghana to be precise – our traditional views on child rearing are very much 'you must be seen and not heard'.

Children are seen (and I speak in general terms – this was not my upbringing) as not having the right ever to comment or give opinions on matters that involve adults.

I recall whenever I got out of line, my mother had a saying she would deliver, and that was: 'Sɛ anantuo yɛ kɛseɛ sen serɛ aa,na yareɛ na ɛwɔ mu!' This was delivered in my native tongue of Twi, meaning, 'If the calf becomes bigger than the thigh, then it can only be due to sickness'. In other words, a child cannot feel they have more wisdom than an adult because an adult has been around longer than a child.

Another one that got thrown around was: 'Sɛ wo papa ne wo maame ɛ tease aa wo, nnyini da': 'For as long as your mother and father are still alive, you will never be grown'.

I think it's pretty clear to see that children in certain cultures are not given the same right to a voice as others; being from certain ethnic backgrounds generally means that you do as you are told.

I also recall someone once saying, 'Obey now and complain later'. This is by no means to say there aren't voiceless children in every society, but this picture is more common in some cultures than others.

Possibly more attention needs to be paid to scenarios like this and more of a conscious effort needs to be made to set the scene for children from these backgrounds to have their voices heard.

The dynamics of how children are allowed to behave and express themselves to adults and parents can affect how these children relate to adults generally.

I remember being in school and having friends that would vamoose as soon as they could hear their father's car's engine coming into the driveway.

There was no relationship there and the only reason you hung around was to say, 'Good evening daddy,' and that was that. No 'how was your day', 'how was school', 'let's sit down and have a catch up' etc.

The parent was the parent and the child was the child – end of story.

Relationships don't just happen; they need to be cultivated and nurtured. We cannot take for granted that we just fall into a good relationship with our kids just because we gave birth to them or adopted them. They will love us, yes, but that doesn't translate, or equate, to being in a great or open and transparent relationship with them.

Admittedly children are born with a 'trust gene' built into their DNA and the only time it stops working is after a lot of disappointments and let downs, and when I say a lot, I mean A

LOT! Why? Because children naturally see the good in people until they sense the bad; their love and trust is unconditional.

When we invest in building closeness to our children and they feel that we value them, not only as human beings but their opinions also, it cultivates an atmosphere of safety. It allows them to be themselves and to speak their mind, knowing they won't be judged or reprimanded for sharing what's in their heart.

And whilst we're on the topic of children being themselves, we must respect their space and allow them to set their own boundaries.

Do you remember being forced to shake a hand or sit on the lap of an aunt or uncle, or kiss a guest who had come to visit when you were a kid?

How uncomfortable did it make you feel?

Why shouldn't you have the right to decline sitting on someone's lap etc. if you don't feel comfortable doing so?

It is totally unacceptable to force a child to make physical contact with anyone if they don't feel comfortable or simply just don't feel like it.

As adults, if we are forced to sit on someone's lap or have to kiss someone we didn't want to or whatever, there would be a name for that! Don't make it suddenly OK because your child can't say no. You must be the voice of your child. Some people mean absolutely no harm when they try and touch your child but really that's irrelevant. Your child should have the right to operate within the boundaries of how they feel most comfortable.

Considering over 90% of sexually abused children are abused by someone they know, wisdom would dictate that you pay attention to your child not wanting to be picked up, tickled, being made to offer kisses or being kissed.

My daughter was always a bit of a snob from when she was born, so she wouldn't go to anyone she didn't like and you couldn't make her either.

I remember when she was little, people would force her to be picked up and she absolutely hated it. Being the firecracker that she is, she would kick so hard that whoever had picked her up would quickly put her down. My daughter would always say she didn't want to be picked up, so why force her?

People soon learnt to give her a high five instead; it was much quieter and a lot less painful on the shins.

There is so much we can learn about our children by just observing them, from knowing anything from their favourite foods to deeper things such as knowing what personality types they are and what makes them tick or what ticks them off.

When we show our children that home is a safe haven, a sanctuary almost, we assure them that everything connected to the home has been considered and set for their safety and wellbeing.

Our relationship with our children is solidified because of the atmosphere we've created, so now when anyone is introduced into the home there is a balance left to the child to reach between the potential of their haven being threatened or pleasing you by accepting the person you have invited into the space they share with you.

Depending on the relationship you have with your child, their age and personality, this will determine how forthright they will be with their opinion or feelings.

The thing to note is if you really study your child, you will know if they're happy or not.

Chapter 8
The Signs...

Emotional intelligence (**EI**) or emotional quotient (**EQ**) is the ability to recognise your own and other people's emotions.

It's the ability to tell the difference between various feelings and categorise them accordingly; EI/EQ therefore enables you to use information derived from emotions to govern and guide thinking and behaviour, as well as to manage and/or adjust emotions to acclimatise oneself to the environment with the objective of reaching a specific destination in regards to emotions.

Being emotionally savvy is a must for any sound relationship, even a relationship with yourself. If we are able to understand feelings or emotions, then we are in a good place to make more informed decisions about why we do the things we do but better still, to prevent doing the things we don't want to do.

Being emotionally aware will also empower us to manage situations around those connected to us, who need our support to navigate through our emotions or allow us to be comfortable in expressing them. Being able to be emotionally free to someone who values our opinions and how we feel is crucial to having and maintaining a healthy connection.

This is especially the case when it comes to children being able to express how they feel about a new partner being brought into the home.

If you are wearing your emotionally savvy hat, you will be able to spot the signs of your child(ren) silently telling you that they aren't happy or feel unsafe.

Children aren't always able to articulate how they feel, in fact they are seldom able to articulate how they feel and often feelings are expressed through behaviour and not words.

Naturally children of different ages and personalities will express themselves in ways unique to who they are, so it's imperative that we are tuned in and wired up so we can hear the voices of our children through their behaviour and more so through their 'misbehaviour'.

Sometimes when children are acting out, we deal with the actions and seldom look at the reason behind the behaviour.

There is a lot for information to look out for and be aware of and it's hard. Admittedly, parenting doesn't come with a manual but knowing what to look out for will make the job much easier.

We are the voices for our children and should be the ultimate authority when it comes to their safety, so let's look at some manifestations in behaviour when children don't feel safe at home.

Obvious signs in younger children:

Reluctant to be alone with your new partner

Recoiling when they try to touch them

Not wanting to talk to them

Being clingy

Crying

General signs of being uncomfortable in their presence

It is also worth mentioning that younger children who are being sexually abused can also exhibit the above signs as well as those listed below:

Becoming withdrawn

Demonstrating sexual behaviours with their toys or objects

Disruptive sleeping patterns including nightmares

Outbursts of anger or overreacting emotionally to minor situations

Unexplainable fear of people or places

Changes in eating habits

In older children where there may be sexual abuse or fear of a new partner, the signs may manifest in the same way as in younger children but in addition the following may also occur:

Becoming withdrawn

Drop in school grades

Misbehaviour in school

Truancy

Getting involved in drink and drugs

Self-harming

Bedwetting

Having expensive gifts that they can't explain where they have come from

Being unusually secretive

Falling ill due to STDs but knowing they aren't sexually active

Falling pregnant

Mood swings and sudden and unexplainable feelings of insecurity

Bleeding and/or bruising around the genital/anal area/ mouth

Again, this list is not exhaustive but gives a good general view of what signs to look out for.

There can be other factors that may contribute to sudden behavioural changes, so it's worth looking at anything that may have changed in your child's life that may explain some of the above.

The important thing is not to feel that you're being silly or overreacting, trust your gut instincts and seek support and help if you have concerns about your child.

It's amazing how much we take for granted when it comes to protecting children.

I had a conversation with a mother who was convinced that her daughter could never be sexually abused because the daughter didn't like being touched near her private parts when being bathed and was 'too confident'.

It's shocking that some parents still feel that their children are empowered to identify and fend off a sexual predator.

What we must realise is that predators of any kind are far more cunning and experienced in their chosen field of abuse than your child is at fending off an abuser.

The areas of sexual grooming and child sexual exploitation is something that all parents need to familiarise themselves with.

If we have a clear understanding of what sexual grooming is, for example, the process and means by which a sexual predator initiates before physically attacking a child will allow a greater degree of protection and knowledge in what signs to spot.

Sometimes it can be really simple things like the offer of babysitting children but with a frequency and eagerness that may cause concern, especially where the child is reluctant to be in the company of that person.

These lists are just a few examples of how your child may exhibit their dislike or sometimes even fear of your new partner.

Of course most young children can show signs of not wanting to interact with a new person, but you have your instincts for a reason. If after a reasonable period of time of interaction around this person, your child doesn't seem to be budging and it's not just that they're being possessive of you, then you need to seriously reconsider if this person should be in your home and around your children.

The truth is, how your child acts is probably just a snapshot or a snippet of a bigger picture. This could be the point that you begin to pay real attention to the other parts of the relationship where there are indicators of who your new man really is. Pay attention and try to look at your relationship from the outside looking in. Seek opinions from trusted and sound-minded members of your family and friends.

Children have instincts too and maybe they're trying to tell you something.

As I said before – often they can see what we can't because

we are so caught up in the euphoria of a new relationship, so we explain away little niggles before really taking time to explore and interpret them.

One of the most common excuses not to pay attention is our 'right to be happy'. Do we have a right to be happy or a right to a life? Absolutely we do, but to what and to whose expense?

Why should your happiness need to have casualties? And why should those casualties be your children?

The cost to a child's emotional, physical and sometimes sexual being is really too high a price to pay – believe me. Too many products of emotional, sexual and psychological abuse were groomed in this kind of an environment.

Getting your groove on for a fleeting moment, more often than not, has a lifelong effect on your children and takes way too long to set your children right long after 'Mr. I Couldn't Do Without You' has gone.

I have said this before and I'll say it again: it is never the responsibility of a 'victim' not to become a victim. It benefits our communities and our society as a whole to take seriously the responsibility to educate, inform and empower our children on issues regarding healthy relationships, understanding sexual responsibility and respecting sexual boundaries. Within this, we need to create enough education around sexual and other types of abuse so that children can feel safe to speak to us about their bodies and hopefully where they feel uncomfortable in someone's company or being able to disclose to a trusted adult about abuse or the threat of it.

Children cannot be expected to control the informed, deliberate and conscious acts of adults; whether it's to dodge the evil clutches of an abusive partner or to suffer the consequences of the choice of their mother to bring the 'unbringable' into their home.

Even in adult relationships, communication is key to a successful union.

Trust is built through relationships. We need to make time for our children and create atmospheres where they feel free to speak about absolutely anything that troubles them without freaking out or even looking shocked.

Admittedly the latter isn't easy. I remember my son talking to me about certain things when he was a teenager; he's 24 now, but there were times my only saving grace was that I wasn't having a cup of tea at the time of our 'mother and son' moments; spitting my tea out all over the kitchen table would have given me away in an instant. I have to be honest though, I was always grateful that he was able to come and speak to me about absolutely anything, no matter how much my toes curled under the table in the process.

Both my children started speaking really early (and they haven't stopped since!) and I remember lying on the bed with my son when he was about three whilst we were on holiday and us just chatting like two old friends. That memory is still with me over twenty years later. Maybe because of this I was able to discuss and teach my son about domestic violence from when he was seven.

There is no magic formula to building love and trust with your children, just speak to them, and if that's hard for you because of your background and where you're coming from, it's never too late to get help and support.

Speak to your kids. Listen to your kids. Believe your kids.

Chapter 9
Who is This Guy?...

First impressions can be as revealing as they can be deceiving, and depending on your state of mind, can show you what you want to see and make you hear what you want to hear.

In everyday interactions, we tend to gravitate towards those with whom we feel some connection or affiliation.

Anything from having the same ethnicity to practising the same religion, marital status, liking the same food, films, books and an array of many other reasons, makes us feel safe and comfortable when someone mirrors the same likes or values as us.

We commend a potential suitor as being on top of his game when he's able to find what makes his prospective love interest tick, in order to impress and win brownie points.

Hopefully the agenda of this man is entirely honourable, and his motive is solely to woo and impress for good reason.

Dinner dates, gifts, compliments? – oooh, the compliments! Isn't it music to our ears to hear the person we're interested in tell us how wonderful we look, how good we smell, how amazingly we cook, etc? Little by little the dependency on these words grow and build us up to feel special, wanted, needed, appreciated and valued.

Such men are normally considered to be a good catch and begin to make our girlfriends jealous and our guy friends checking how they measure up.

These are the kind of guys the smart ladies don't want to let get away.

They create a sense of security with their words and actions that break down defences. You feel like it's time to exhale, that your heart can finally come home to rest.

But there's another type of man...

He masquerades as the one just described but with a very different agenda.

His modus operandi is to woo, compliment, build up.

He knows that if you've never been treated like a queen or if you have heard his smooth words before, you've never really believed you were worthy of them.

You never felt that such words were confirmation of what you already knew or believed of yourself because these words were words of affirmation, not confirmation! For a man whose intentions are to break you down and capture you, there's a stark difference in the spirit behind the words he speaks into your soul.

There is a pattern every predatory man uses, and that's to lull the unsuspecting female into a false sense of security.

There is a very clear process of operation and execution, which starts with gainining confidence and trust. Then once he's got you where he wants you, you're isolated and then the rest is history...

When you aren't sure of who you are or you have such emotional needs and voids that you're so eager to please and not be jilted, you may not even realise the wheels of motion that have been put in place.

The wooing by a predatory man is done with an agenda in mind, and that is to make you drop your guard or make you forget that you should have one.

His sole objective is to capture you – mentally, emotionally, financially, physically and sometimes sexually – by presenting himself as being all that you initially want and need, but what you end up feeling you cannot possibly do without or get rid of.

The emotional and mental dependency acts as the foundation and catalyst that enables him to capture all your limiting beliefs about yourself and your power of choice, so as to give himself free reign to subdue and overpower you mentally and emotionally.

Their objective for treating you like a queen is to eventually make you their peasant slave by the dependency they create.

Neither this man nor the person that manifests in you is easily identifiable, because the mask drops off for him and the garments of togetherness and wholeness drops off from you.

Who you both really are reveals itself in time, and the real characters in the play are revealed, the real relationship begins; the predator has captured his prey.

I speak a lot about what our needs are as human beings and further narrowed down as women, and one thing I've come to realise is that life is better lived when happiness or contentment isn't tied to one particular thing or part of our lives.

When we are able to live a full life, it allows us to live life at its peak in various areas, so emphasis on one particular area being the sole source of validation or success doesn't have the power to topple us when that area doesn't yield the fruits that we expect, when and how we expect it.

There's a popular tool life coaches use called the 'Wheel of Life', where the wheel is divided usually into six or eight sections covering areas such as: family, relationships, finances, health and fitness, career, personal growth, social life and spiritual life.

The areas covered may have slight variations depending on the coach but essentially these are the main areas you'll normally be asked to look at and rate from a scale of 1 to 10, to determine your feelings and assessment of where you are in your life.

The areas that score on the lower end of the scale are usually the first areas the coach will work on with you.

Interestingly, I have had some clients who have come to me in total despair of 'everything going wrong', but on closer inspection, after exploring the different areas of my clients lives, it quickly becomes apparent that the one area of concern isn't indicative of all others being in a bad place.

It's natural that the area of concern would jump out, but if you allow yourself to have other interests and not allow relationships to be the only thing on your Wheel of Life, you will be better equipped to make better assessments on love relationships and not allow that area to totally rule and dominate everything else.

We all like to be told nice things. We all enjoy a little ego massage from time to time and these men know that.

'Flattery will get you everywhere'… I would be very surprised if anyone reading this hasn't come across this saying.

I wouldn't be surprised if every predatory male has this phrase in his bag of tricks.

I came across a definition of flattery as being: 'An excessive and insincere praise, given especially to further one's own interest'.

There are so many elements to our existence that we can build up and create healthy 'distractions' until a natural manifestation appears where we want it. By being in that head space, there really won't be too much opportunity for the insincere amongst us to woo us with words that are steeped in insincerity for their 'own interests'.

Look in the mirror and affirm who you are by vocalising the great things about you, and if you can't find anything good to say about yourself, what do people say about you? Has no one ever paid you a compliment? Has no one ever said anything good to you or about you?

Well here's one for you: if you're reading this book, then you're obviously alive. Life isn't something everyone has the luxury of experiencing. You being alive means you have a chance denied to many. It means so far, you've made it. It means you have a blessing someone somewhere has been denied but granted to you because there's still something you still need to do on this planet.

Life may be extremely difficult right now, but where there is life there is hope and it is my sincere desire to help give you that.

You're brave in wanting to change the course of how you apply yourself in this life, by taking the chance to want to do life differently; that is commendable and I commend you.

Chapter 10
The Reality...

You will find here a collection of four true life stories.

These stories are unedited to keep the authenticity of what you are about to read.

The stories are painful and disturbing and go into great detail. Some of you may find what you are about to read distressing so I apologise in advance for this, but not for the truth that you are about to hear.

These ladies have chosen to share these parts of their lives and their journeys because every one of them felt that their stories mattered. They believed that by speaking up they could help save a woman, a girl, a man, a boy, from the heartache and pain they have been forced to endure.

They don't want pity, because pity wasn't the motivation behind them taking the decision to share their experiences of child abuse, rape and domestic violence.

The belief that speaking up is their part in disarming the power of the past over their lives is what has motivated them to share.

I know it hasn't been easy for any of them.

My asking them to speak about things that have been buried, to be exhumed and an autopsy performed on their life experiences on cue was particularly hard, and even I didn't appreciate how difficult it was going to be; I have apologised for that.

I requested the ladies to take their time, to throw timescales out of the window and speak and write at their own pace – they did it.

So to you? My only request is that you read these stories without prejudice or judgement, and take from it the knowledge they wish to impart, if not for you, for the woman next to you. The woman next to you who may be experienced in wearing a mask that will only slip when she feels it's safe to do so.

Please find a quiet spot and proceed...

Chapter 11

Malia's Story – In The Shadows...

'Hi, my name is Malia, I'm 42 years old.

'I'm Hispanic.

'This is really hard, I don't know how I'm gonna do this. Aaaarggggh!' (whispers) 'Damn.'

(she gives a deep sigh)

'Let me see the question.

'I didn't grow up with my blood father; I grew up with my step-father from five till thirteen.

'Uhm, the abuse started almost instantly, it was physical at first, with him beating us with belts and rulers and stuff like that. Then it turned into us having to,' (deep sighs again) 'pretty much always having to strip naked to get beat.

'Uhm, pretty much blocked out that he wasn't my real dad until I was twelve when I started having flashbacks, so I always thought this guy was my dad, so I thought it was normal.

'Uhm, at first it was just me and my older brother dealing with it.

'When I turned about six, my younger brother came to stay with us, he moved from South America to came to stay with us, and that's when it got really... disgusting.

'Uhm, basically, this guy used to... I'm gonna just get right into it 'cos I don't wanna have to stay here longer than I have to be.

'He pretty much would have us strip naked, me and my younger brother only, and touch each other… so my first experience with a guy was with my brother.

'He would watch us and show everyone what to do.

'Uhm, it got to the point where Larry and I would lock ourselves in the room and I would beg my mum to come home but she wouldn't.

'She pretty much figured that, it was the sacrifice she took… she told me later on it was a sacrifice we paid to have nice things and to have a house… yeah…

'I remember, around ten I started to put bleach… in his food to try to get rid of him so he wouldn't do it to us any more, uhm, this lasted for, for about a year and a half and he started getting really sick. Bad ulcers and throwing up blood and all that so I finally told my mum what was going on. And I told her that she needs to leave him or I'd kill him and tell the police that she made me do it.

'So she finally walked away and left him; ONLY because of that, not because she wanted to.

'My brother ended up worse than me.

'I was able to somewhat cope with what had happened for those few years. He on the other hand wasn't able to cope. He still felt mentally like he was supposed to be with me… sexually, so I had to separate myself from him because he didn't know not to touch me in certain ways.

'Uhm… every now and then he'll still try, it's usually when he's intoxicated that he'll try to go back there and relive what we used to do.' (Malia sighs long and deeply)

'My mother, she never even got touched or abused or anything so she pretty much just let us take the fall for her.

'Uhm… around thirteen I also had confronted him and started having flashbacks and let him know he wasn't my dad.

'He didn't like that too much. He got really violent, but, uhm, I ended up running away from home right after that because he was still in the picture. Even though she left him, he was still in the picture so I ran away from home around thirteen.

'Uhm, I got married really early just as a, I guess, just a way to escape? But I ended up with people who used to cheat on me and then I had a boyfriend who used to beat the crap out of me.

'He ended up, this is like, we spent like two years together. I got pregnant but he beat me, up, so bad that I ended up losing a set of twins; I was almost five months pregnant.

'I was able to leave him and ended up getting married again and I was with him for a few years, fourteen years actually and had somewhat of a normal family, but I was so paranoid that I didn't let him deal with his kids because I was afraid that he was going to do it to them, even though he never showed any signs of that.

'We ended up breaking up and then I was attacked at gunpoint at a gas station and raped. Seems like I'm a magnet for that now. I still have nightmares. I still have really bad nightmares.

'I've tried to commit suicide twice and both times I've ended up in ICU for over a week. Uhm, I have severe depression.

'I'm supposed to be on medication but I'm not right now.

'Every day is a struggle.

'…I don't know what else to say…' (long pause… long deep sigh)

'I don't sleep well at night. I have severe nightmares and I have a phobia of people touching me; like I really can't form a connection.

'My ex actually broke up with me over it, because I couldn't be intimate without being completely covered and the lights had to be completely off because I couldn't look at him, plus I didn't want him looking at my body; when I was raped the man ended up burning my body with cigarettes so I have like fifty cigarette marks all over my back and legs and body so, to see it really affects me so I can't… look at them.

'Uhm, seems like I can't really get close to people any more.

I don't trust anybody. I'm very paranoid. I pretty much robbed my kids of a childhood 'cos I was too afraid to let them spend the night at people's houses.

'I don't feel I'm ever gonna be happy or gonna be free of this, 'cos this has happened so many times for so long, and then my mother won't admit anything happened!

'All she says is it was a sacrifice we have to pay, but she won't admit what actually happened.

'Uhm… luckily I grew up not to let anything happen to my kids. My kids have never been abused. They're all very healthy. My daughter has never had to deal with anything like that, so for that I'm grateful but as far as my life? I really don't have one.

'Pretty much stay a prisoner in the house. I don't really like to leave.'

(Long pause)

'Yeah… what affected me the worst was the childhood stuff. That stayed with me. Really, really bad.

'I don't know what else to say right now.

'It took me four days just to say this, so… If you need more I guess you can ask me, but right now I just can't. I'm sure there's more you need to know. I just don't know how to pull it out. I need more questions.

Bye.'

It's over a week and Malia hasn't been able to speak to me about this. I have felt physically and emotionally drained listening to the despair in her voice at times and the struggle to speak the words. Some sentences she rushes really quick as if she doesn't want the words to make her mouth dirty.

I've told her to take her time.

She's agreed for us to work together because she said she trusts me.

I'm waiting for the rest of her story.

Malia came back to me after two weeks to finish telling me what she had experienced in her childhood and the experiences she has had as an adult:

'I think I'll start all over again.

'My earliest memory, I think I was about five. I remember this house in some sort of suburb and we lived in a four-bedroom house with a backyard.

'We were never allowed outside at the back. We had like a black housekeeper who used to follow behind me to make sure I never got dirty 'cos if I got dirty I would get beat up really bad, so she was pretty much turned into a mum figure. She would make us extra food, candy and stuff like that and she would always try and make sure, like at least a little bit of fun before what I now know to be my stepfather at the time.

'I actually blocked him out. His name was Gerry; he was the reason my mum left South America to come here.

'So let me backtrack a little bit, let me backtrack a little bit: My mum basically stole me and my two brothers from my father when she met this white man named Gerry. She left one day to go do some errands and never returned, from what I gather from the rest of my family… she stole us out of the country with this man. She forged all of our paperwork, brought us into America and once he got her here, he basically made her like a slave. She just basically had to do everything he told her to do. This went on for let me say a year, then one day my brother and I decided to go into his room, we were babies, five and six and we ate something we shouldn't have touched, and we ate his chocolates that he had on his counter.

'Well I don't remember her name but the housekeeper ran in and said we're gonna be in a lot of trouble. She told us to just stay in our room until they got home and try to stay away from him. Now when he got home he came after us, he was drunk and he came after us, and I guess my mum was so afraid that he was gonna kill us that she ran out the house with us and we had to hide under her on top of a car because some dogs came after us to attack us. So finally we got away and she ended up… I don't know where she ended up actually, because I don't remember much after that, but I know that a year later we're in Texas and I remember being in day care and having another guy pull up in a black car, picked us up and from that day, he was always there – he was our new dad.

'OK… and that's when I started being abused by the new guy. The guy used to sexually abuse me. Used to beat me up pretty good and I remember having cleft palate surgery and coming home from the hospital. Mind you, back then, when they used to do these surgeries they'd have to dislocate your jaw, slice up your whole throat, then stitch you up and wire your jaw shut, so you're on a strict liquid diet or pudding, Jello or stuff like that.

'Well, it was like two days after the surgery, I had wanted real food 'cos I was hungry and I guess I kept harassing him and he made it for me but after trying to eat it, I realised it hurt too much; I was probably like seven years old at this point… I was seven years old. It hurt so much that I couldn't eat it, so he was angry and said since I made it for you, you are gonna eat it. He made me sit there and eat all of it. It went all down my throat and I had to go back into surgery the next day.

'So I was able to get away from that guy. It was kind of weird… uhm… I was also very anorexic, so I would hide food or if I was forced to eat food I would vomit and if I vomited in the garbage can, he would make me scoop it out and eat it; I remember that happened a lot. I would get to the point where I would pretty much hide food all around the house until he would go to sleep then I would throw it away because he would actually make me eat it out of the garbage can or if I threw up in the garbage or if I threw it out, he would make me eat my vomit… uhm… he, he had an alcohol problem and he would drink a lot. He would never touch my mum, never hurt her but he would hit me and my brothers. He would hit us with everything and we pretty much lived like we were in prison. Every day we had to clean, even if the house was clean we had to clean and he would walk around with a white glove test and everything that had dust, we would get beat pretty hard for it and I'm not talking about one spanking or two spankings – I'm talking about pretty much twenty, thirty times with a wooden ruler across my hands until they bled.

'I remember my brother was running one day and he tripped and I was right next to him and just out of, it wasn't out of malice or anything, it was reflexes. When he went to fall he grabbed me by the hair by accident and he happened to rip out two handfuls of my hair because my hair was down to my knees. It was just a reflex. He went to grab onto me but grabbed my hair by accident and he ripped out a handful of hair. I wasn't crying or anything. It didn't hurt but my stepfather saw that and counted every hair and hit him for every last hair... with a leather strap. My mum never stepped in, never stopped him. She allowed it 'cos it was our sacrifice for having a nice house and expensive things; that was her reasoning behind it.

'Uhm... I remember we used to run away a lot and when we'd come back he would really beat us. I remember him going into the shower for my brother and beating him so bad, I remember it looked like somebody was murdered in the shower, but the worst part of it was, was him making me touch my younger brother. He never made me touch my older brother but he always made me and my younger brother do things we shouldn't be doing together... sexually, kissing, touching... it was really disgusting... uhm... About nine, ten, we moved to Florida with him and my mum and stuff continued here. It just got to the point that basically I was his housewife. I would have to cook for him, I would have to clean for him, I would have to iron out his clothes whilst my mum just had like the best life; she didn't have to do anything. So... my older brother ended up having to run away and they found him overdosed, well, almost dead in a Walgreens bathroom, which is a grocery store here in Florida. He had drunk a bottle of Draino. He wanted to die and took two bottles of Draino, one into the bathroom right before they closed and drank the two bottles of Draino and they still don't understand because Draino has metal strands in it to help break up clogs. Somehow he was able to drink almost the whole two bottles and he ended up in hospital for like seven months.

'After he recovered they put him in a mental hospital so then that left me and my younger brother alone and he used to help us a lot, he used to take a lot of the beatings for us so we wouldn't have to take it, so when he left, things got really bad for me and my brother 'cos now we had nobody there to protect us. Well my younger brother and I became alcoholics by about twelve. We would drink every night. We would go to the local minimart, steal whatever we could steal and at night we would just drink, so we wouldn't have to think of it anymore.

'Well my younger brother decided he was going to leave too and he left me by myself with my stepfather. He ran away and never came back either so I was left... and I started to put bleach in his food, especially when he was drunk I would put bleach in his drinks and I tried to kill him and this went on for about a year and he was getting very sick and was going to the hospital a lot, but this was mid-eighties so back then they didn't have all the stuff they do now. So he was coughing up blood, very sick, losing a lot of weight and they couldn't figure out what was wrong with him, so I finally confessed to my mum that, you know, I was trying to kill him because of her letting him do all those things to us and finally that gave me some courage that I ended up leaving and running away from home.

'About a year after I left home, I met up with my brothers again and we ended up doing a lot of illegal things to survive and I'm talking about a fourteen-year-old, a thirteen-year-old and a fifteen-year-old. We're stealing from stores and robbing people for money... just to survive. So that went on for two, three years until I saw something on the news of some young guy that we knew got shot and was killed and I got scared and didn't want my brothers to get hurt, so I made them all stop what we were doing and we all got crappy little jobs here and there and we took care of each other until I got older and you know, ended up married. Uhm... I didn't have the best adult life either because I dated a guy that used to beat the crap out of me. Uhm... we would do that for about three years.

'I would ask my mum if I could come stay with her because I needed to get away from him, and she would tell me, "No!" It was not her business, not her problem, so I would have to stay with him... uhm, I stayed with him for three years until, actually – let me go back, let me go back.

'When I was sixteen, I was raped by my boyfriend. I told my mum what had happened, that I was pregnant and we went to confront his father with it. His father was a cop. His father didn't really care about it. He said, "It is what it is. You're already pregnant so you're gonna keep it." He basically said if I got rid of the kid then he would set my brothers up with drugs, so that that way they could go to jail, so he made me pretty much always come to the house. I was still his son's girlfriend and I just had to play that role. So without letting them know, I had a friend help me with money and I went and had an abortion, which I still regret to this day, but I had an abortion to get away from him. I just told them I lost it.

'I was able to get away from that guy. It was kinda weird.

'My stepfather that used to make us do all that weird stuff and do all that nasty stuff, his name is Larry, the guy that raped me at sixteen – his name was Larry. My younger brother who I had to do all those sexual things with, his name is Larry... That's weird... I never thought about that. So after I got away from my boyfriend, you know, things got a little bit better for me. I met someone that was really good to me. We were each other's best friends but when we got older we weren't able to be around each other too much so things went downhill after that.

'I met my kids' dad. We ended up having the kid and having these children and one night I found out that he was cheating on me. He was out of town with some girl the night I got taken by gunpoint at a gas station and was raped by a complete stranger and he had me for about four and a half hours and he beat me so bad that I almost died.

I was in the hospital and they told my mom from the hospital that she needed to come. She wasn't there more than three minutes when the police escorted her out and told her she can't come back and the reason that was, was because I'm lying there all black and blue and bloody, and the first thing that came out of her mouth was, "What did you do to cause this?" So that made the deputies really upset and they made her leave... so I was in the hospital for about a week, when I got out the hospital I went home and my husband had told me I was dirty and disgusting, even though it wasn't my fault that he didn't really want me touching the children because he didn't know if I had something now, didn't want me kissing my own kids and then when I got out the hospital, his mother called me and told me that I need to suck it up and told me that I was not the first person to ever be raped and I won't be the last, so suck it up and leave and stop crying about it, and this is the day I got out of the hospital – mind you she has a daughter and she had no problem telling me that, so I got out the hospital. That same day my husband decides to go out to a club with the same girl that he cheated on me with. That same night. And then his mum tells me that I have a week to pretty much find somewhere else to live.

'So I pretty much snapped and this night about ten o'clock, the grocery store by the house, I bought as many sleeping pills as I could, and I waited until one in the morning and went behind the same store, behind the same plaza to go take them, 'cos I figured you know, at that point it would be closed and nobody would find me until morning.

'So I went back there and took all these pills and I don't know if you've heard, but if you take a certain amount of pills your body starts to reject them. I was able to put down like four or five boxes. Even though it was very hard, it took a long time and my body just wanted to reject them but I was just forcing them down, almost to the point where I was gagging.

'So they started to take effect really fast. The last thing I remember someone screaming at me, "What did you take, what did you take?" Come to find out now, it was the paramedic, and what they told me is that it happened that it was only about a mile trip to the plaza from the hospital so it wouldn't have taken more than three minutes to the hospital from where I was but they had to revive me about four times because I kept dying.

'It turns out that the plaza had a twenty-four-hour dialysis service inside of it and I didn't know that. They have like dark windows so you can't really tell that they're open, so I guess an employee had gone behind the building to go smoke 'cos he wasn't allowed to do it in front of the building so he went to the back of the building to smoke and he found me, and he called 911.

'So a week later, about a week and a half later in ICU with a tube down my throat 'cos I wasn't breathing on my own so they had a thing to make me.

'When I woke up I had this loud Jamaican nurse who cussed me out and told me I almost died and that, you know, I shouldn't do stupid things like that.

'Then she went and told me that, "You had this one poor guy by your bedside crying his eyes out every day. Every single day you had this poor guy crying for you. Like you must've really scared him 'cos he thought you were gonna die." So I asked her if my husband was here. And she was like, "Yeah, he was here every day crying." And when she told me his name, it wasn't my husband. My husband never came to see me… not one day, neither did my mom, so they never came to the hospital; nobody either side came to my side. They actually told my kids that I had gotten sick and was in the hospital but was contagious so they couldn't go see me.

'The guy that was there checking up on me, was actually my ex-husband's best friend, somebody I didn't even like. Me and him, all we did was argue every time we were around each other. We didn't even like each other at all. But when he heard (his mother's a nurse) that apparently she heard about what happened and she told him that, "Nobody comes to see her," so he came in the first time to see me, and mind you he has a very strong phobia of hospitals since his dad died in the hospital, but yet he still made it to the hospital.

'He came to see me the first day and felt so bad that he came every single day and sat there for hours, talking to me... so when I got out the hospital, I was told that I needed to leave 'cos I couldn't stay at the hospital anymore 'cos not only am I dirty, but I'm also crazy. So the guy Olivier, the one who came to see me at the hospital, he lived with his mother at the time, and they had a three bedroom townhouse, and they both invited me to come stay with them and I ended up staying with them for a while because I still didn't have my kids – I still couldn't be with them. They allowed me to come visit but that was it, but he didn't let me stay with my kids, so I stayed at Olivier's house 'cos it was only like ten minutes away from my kids.

'My mom didn't let me stay with her either, so I had no other option but to be there. So after that, I finally got my kids back, about a year later I got my kids back but the depression was so bad that I couldn't have them 'cos I couldn't get over it, I didn't really have the time to deal with it, never had the time to deal with it. Nobody ever gave me the chance so I was still very sick and very... mentally not right. So about a year later I sent my kids, not to go live with their dad but I sent them there for the day 'cos I already had a plan that I would finish the job this time? And so I sent them... I wrote each kid a letter to find after I was dead. I sent my kids to their dad's house and I left again... and I had an idea 'cos you know, I knew how long it took for the pills to take effect the first time.

'So I took these pills and then was gonna drive to the beach but the pills this time took effect whilst I was driving, really fast; I wasn't expecting that, I actually passed out at the wheel.

'I'm still really mad at myself for that 'cos I could've hurt somebody really bad.

'What happened, this is what I was told by the cop:

'Uhm... I passed out at the wheel at a very busy intersection, and there was like a mini highway and I passed out and somehow my car coasted through the intersection, avoided all the cars that almost hit me and stopped like a foot from his police car, passed out, dead.

'He, uhm... rushed me to the hospital and I don't know, he must've felt really bad 'cos I had the letters in the car with me and he must've read them and he felt really bad and what he ended up reporting it as was, he reported it as a seizure, a mild seizure and told the nurses not to – I guess he had connections in the hospital. He told the nurses not to write down the level of drugs in my system so I wouldn't go to jail. He didn't want me to go to jail; he just wanted me to get help so I have no record because of him, 'cos that would have been considered a DUI. And uhm... I forgot what other charges he said it was... negligence or something like that 'cos I put all those people in danger. Luckily he said nobody hit me and nobody got hurt, but because of him I don't have a record so...

'I didn't go to the mental hospital after that, he did have me "Baker Acted", which basically means the State can put you in the hospital. Again nobody came to see me that time either, uhm... yeah... I was in the hospital that time for like two weeks 'cos I had a lot of damage, really screwed up my liver and a lot of damage... uhm, yeah... after that, I was alone for a little while. I didn't take my kids back because didn't want... I was still suicidal so I didn't want my kids around me; I let them go live with their dad again.

'I saw them every two days. I took them to all their football and basketball and cheerleading practices. I would go to all the cheerleading practices; I was very involved – I just could not live with them because I was afraid that night would be the night that I decide to do something and they would find me. But I was still very active in their life, that's why now that they're older they understand what was going on. They don't hold grudges and they're not mad because they understand that at least I was still trying to be there.

'So that's why we're still very close. I never abandoned them, just thought it was safer for them to be at their dad's house, to sleep.

'So... fast forward to a few years later, I decided I would go to culinary school – I still had no help so at this point I'm living in my car, my van because I couldn't work, I just couldn't do anything, just a recluse almost. I was afraid to be around people.

'So I went to culinary school, I put myself through culinary school while living out of my car and I got a gym membership so I could have a shower and I ate at school 'cos it was a culinary school.

'I graduated, my kids were all there when I graduated and then I started doing better… I started doing better and my kids were with me again and things were going OK.

'A few years in, I met a guy call Rich; he seemed like the perfect guy until he started beating the crap out of me.

'Rich used to beat me up on a regular basis. He was very big and very scary.

'I tried to get away a few times and I asked my mom, "Hey, can I come stay with you for a little bit so he won't know where I'm at," and she said, "NO!"… It was my problem and I had to deal with it.

'So, he wouldn't really let us use protection but he would always tell me he was being careful and I ended up getting pregnant by him and it was the scariest thing in the world to be pregnant by him 'cos I knew he'd have control over me for the next eighteen years of my life.

'So I stopped eating… I didn't wanna have these kids. I was terrified to be stuck to this man so I stopped eating and I was drinking like a fish. I was scared; I was trying to just self-medicate… uhm… I started getting really sick, I ended up finding out I was pregnant with twins – a boy and a girl.

'So around five months I was driving him to work, he would make me drive him to work and pick him up. And I was driving him to work and I started bleeding. So we went to the hospital.

'They took me to the back and they made him wait in the lobby till they checked me out and I started having a miscarriage, but they were able to… 'cos I was nearly five months there was a way for them to stop it and be able to save the kids.

'But because he wasn't in the room at the time, he was still in the lobby waiting for me to get checked, I had to ask the nurse, "Can you just let them die?" which is really sick and really cruel but… I knew I would've ended up dead if I had to stay with him. So I spoke to the nurse and I showed her you know, I had bruises everywhere on my body that were hidden and I told her please let them go. I told them he beats me up every day and he drinks like a fish. One day he's gonna kill me if I stay with him. That means if I have his kids he has rights so she went back and brought the doctor into the room and she told the doctor what was happening.

'I was waiting for them to tell me they can't do that because of their ethics codes that they have to follow and I was waiting for them to stop it from happening. When the doctor told me OK, we're gonna let this happen, but you can't say this to anybody 'cos I'll lose my license, and I swore to them that I'd never say it to anybody 'cos I didn't want him to get in trouble. But he brought in Rich and told him there was nothing that he could do to save 'em 'cos the kids were already dead, I was gonna have to have a D&C to have them removed because they were poisoning me; that's basically what he told him. So that man cried… 'cos he really wanted those kids and he really wanted to be stuck to me forever and I couldn't allow that to happen.

'I have a lot of guilt for all these things that have happened but I had to save my own life, I know I had to save my own life, but I still feel very guilty for letting that happen.

'So… that night we went back home after I pretty much lost them and had to have the D&C and what the D&C does is it scrapes out your uterus so there's no particles that could rot inside of you.

'So I had the D&C and went home but apparently he was still angry with me that I lost them so he decided to get really drunk that night and he came home. When we got home, he was really upset, and we came in the house when we got back and I guess we didn't lock the door; as soon as we walked through the door he had hit me.

'We started fighting and he hit me so hard that I flew against the wall and the neighbor lady came running into our apartment and she ran in. She opened the door and ran in, didn't care. She had a knife and told him to step away from me or she was gonna stab him. So he actually left. He went a few doors down to go and hang out with his friends. Well I packed my stuff up really quick, whatever I could grab and I jumped in my car; the neighbour, she watched out for me while I got in my car and left. I slept in my van for about a month.

'I asked my mom if I could come back and stay with her 'cos I need somewhere to stay, you know. She kept telling me no but probably would've kept saying no 'cos I'd threatened to tell her church she was letting me sleep on the street, just 'cos she didn't wanna deal with me. So I basically had to blackmail her to stay with her 'cos I was afraid to sleep in the car every night.

'This was a woman that grew up in, like, the perfect family.

'She had like the perfect dad and the perfect mom and from her own accounts, she had like the best childhood. And she had eleven sisters and two brothers and they all tell me the same thing; they all had the perfect childhood.

'All her sisters and brothers grew up to be really good parents. All their kids are super tight with them; not her...

'I can't tell you the last time I heard her say "I love you" or even try or attempt to hug me. I don't even think she ever has to tell you the truth, which is really sad 'cos when I had my kids she was very jealous of that and would always tell my kids not to be all over me all the time. "Stop hugging your mum so much, it's annoying." Because my kids and me are very, very close.

'So the good thing is that, well actually – my kids, I kind of robbed them of their childhood for the simple fact that all the bad things that happened to me, I was so scared to let them go to sleepovers, be around people that I kept them very close to me which I kind of feel bad now... they had a good childhood, they just didn't get to do the stuff regular kids get to do.

'I was also overly paranoid, so that's affected me to the point where I'm a recluse. I really don't like to leave the house, I have these visions of really bad things happening to my kids, like I'll ask people: "Does that mean I want something to happen to them, am I mentally crazy or is there something wrong with me?"

'From what I gather is that I'm just so overly aware of the world I'm just afraid something is going to happen so I'm always having these bad thoughts, not that I, I wanna hurt my kids, I know I would never hurt my kids; I'm just always afraid what happened to me is gonna happen to them.

'Uhm… I tried to confront my mom about all the stuff that happened with her husband and how she never defended us, how she never protected us and she just went from telling us that was the price to pay to now saying it never happened.

'It went from saying, yeah it happened but at least you had somewhere to sleep, you had money, you had food to now, it just never happened; she won't even acknowledge it now.'

(Long pause) 'So I don't know… I feel like it just keeps happening and happening to me. I'm not destined to be happy, ever, this is why I can't be with anybody. It's like, I don't trust people at all. I don't trust men at all. I don't trust females, I don't trust nobody; the only people I trust is my kids. It's just a really, really sad and depressing life.

'Honestly like… I'm really still not over it. I still don't wanna be here…

'I know that if I go my daughter is gonna be next. All my kids have panic attacks.

'They all have depression. They all tell me they had a really good life but yet up to this point but yet they still all suffer from depression and my daughter told me that if anything ever happened to me, she would kill herself. So now I am forced to live here in this world just because I don't want to be just because I don't want her to hurt herself… it's so unfair because I know they'll probably be better off without me anyways!

'… I just wanna be happy and I don't know how to do that…

'I can't be with anybody 'cos I have scars from when I was raped. I've got like over fifty cigarette burns all over my body from this bastard burning me for four hours so any time I consider dating somebody, at some point they're gonna want more and I'm gonna have to show them this and I don't want to, I don't want to, I don't want them to look at me like I'm disgusting… I don't know… I just don't know how anybody can allow this crap to happen to their kid 'cos if this wouldn't have happened as a kid, all the extra stuff wouldn't have happened to me. I've just never had happiness… ever…' (Malia begins to cry) 'My whole life has been miserable.'

'It's just so unfair. I try to be nice to everybody, I try to be good to everybody and no matter how good of a person I am, the worst things happen to me, and continue to keep happening.

'I just don't know how to stop it. I feel like a prisoner in my own body. I don't know… I don't know what else to say.

'I just know that I would never let anything ever happen to my kids. NEVER. I'd protect them with my own life and I just don't understand why she couldn't do that for me.

'I got robbed of normal things that people should get. I've never had real love from anybody.' (Malia whispers quietly) 'I don't know.

'My thoughts of how I feel right now today is: if I could do whatever I wanted to do this second, I would actually probably just drive away and never come back.

'My kids don't have a real mom. They have… I help them to pay their bills, I take care of them, I give them what they need but they have this depressed, sad, pathetic woman as a mom.

'Even in situations where people should be happy, I'm not.

'Birthday parties, Christmas, get-togethers, dinners, everybody's laughing and everybody's joking around and I can't, I can't make myself be happy.

'I really feel like I'm drowning, and nobody understands…' (Malia begins to cry again) 'Everybody just keeps saying, 'Oh you're crazy, you're crazy,' but nobody wants to help me feel better. Everybody wants to laugh at me and make jokes, and laugh at me. My friends are only around me when I can help them, when I can do something for them but when I need them, there's nobody ever around.

'I feel ugly, I feel stupid... I just don't wanna really be here anymore, I really don't.

'Every day is just a struggle to wake up, to get up and all I really wanna do is go away... and I just don't know how to get it out of my head. I don't know what else to do...' (Malia gives a really long deep sigh) 'total despair, almost.

'I DON'T KNOW WHAT ELSE TO DO!'

Chapter 12
Margarita's Story –
On My Own...

'I am 42 years old; I'll be 43 in March.

'I am Mexican American. I was born here in California and my parents were born in Mexico.

'Relationship with my father: Right now, and I'm hoping this will remain forever, I have absolutely no contact with my family. Not one person in my family and I hope to keep it that way because of the abuse in the family. So, but growing up, the relationship I had with my father was kind of bittersweet. I know that my father admired me. He knew that I was very persistent, persevered, resilient.

'He knew that if I put my mind to something I would get it done and he knew that if something needed to get done or if someone needed to figure something out, it would always be me.

'Top student, high IQ, top of everything. Academics, athletically, everything, I could do it all, I could figure it out all, BUT, at the same time, uhm... my mother was very abusive to me. My mother didn't care for me from the time I was born.

'My father worked two full time jobs for fifteen years to put us through Catholic school. So my mother was a bully.

My mother was abusive, my mother was a bully. She had my brother and my sister. My sister's four years older than me, my brother's two years younger than me; she manipulated them into being bullies to me.

'Uhm, very abusive and very, you know, passive aggressive, very narcissistic. My mom just has a lot of issues and so of course, eventually you start to kind of act out. You start to defend yourself and of course, no one would see why I was doing what I was doing. It wasn't that I was a troubled child, I was defending myself, but like to this day everybody covers for my mom so everybody hides and protects her. So of course my father gets home, hears stories about, you know, my either getting into a fight with my brother or my sister or you know, crying all day or just whatever my mom didn't like or I did – uhm, then my father would come home and get tired of it and says he was just tired of hearing of all the complaints about me and then I would get beat by my dad.

'Uhm… so of course you know, I spent my whole life telling my father, "You don't know what goes on in this home, you don't know what goes on in this home," and my father would just shake his head and insist. His famous line was, "There's no way that one person could be right and everybody wrong, that just can't happen, that you're telling me the truth and three other people are lying, that just wouldn't happen!"

'Uhm… it's funny because when I was about in seventh grade, a therapist told him that could happen, and why is it impossible that three people could get together and cover up and lie and this one person is telling the truth, and my dad never said this again. But then that argument changed to, "But you want me to pick and choose between my daughter and my wife." And some of the last words I said to my father when we ended the relationship was, "I don't want you to pick and choose and that's been your problem your whole life. You've failed as a father because you're not just a husband; you're a father and being a husband and father is not about picking one and sticking to that, regardless of what your partner does for you. Regardless of what your child does for you, you don't pick one and support it, regardless of how horrible it is. It's not about picking and choosing wife or daughter, it's about choosing right over wrong, period! But for some reason you refuse to do that."

'Uhm, so my mother, when my father retired, my mother started abusing my father too... uhm, and even when I've stepped in to defend my father, my father would turn on me for upsetting my mom because in his eyes, it's just causing more problems; just let her be. Just let her be abusive, just let her be crazy, just let her be this and that. Because that's what family does! And family doesn't do that. I don't know any relationship that should do that.

'You don't abuse people and you don't cover up for them, uhm... and you don't put up with it and that's why I'm this horrible person, is because I don't stay quiet about it, because I don't put up with it because I don't accept it. I don't cover it up. Uhm, so the relationship between my father and I has been one of, like I said, had it not been for the abuse I think I would've... I think would've gone very far with the support of my father because he saw a lot in me that my mother didn't want to or didn't care about. But because he chose to support the abuse from my mother, he went as far as to become abusive himself with me... and I've had a lot of anger and hatred towards him for that. Because what person, especially because the gender stereotype that your father protects you no matter what. Your father is your hero... your father is the first example of how a man is supposed to treat you... and what I got from that was: He'll protect his own interest and he'll turn on you. And he'll betray you. And he'll hurt you to please others' (she begins to cry) 'and it's funny, 'cos as I'm saying this, I'm realising that it's a pattern I've had... with men... and relationships... my whole life, that either that's what I've had or that's what I expect from them.' (she pauses) 'Oh my goodness! OK, again, the relationship with my mother; uhm... some of the first words my mother said to me, I remember she said to me... uhm, as a child. My childhood memories, she would say to me, in Spanish, and they sounded worse in Spanish, but she would say and these are my memories: "Do not call me mother." It was, OK... it was: Call me 'trash', call me 'whore', call me 'bitch', call me 'dog'. Call me whatever you want but do not call me "mother".

'And she was always constantly reminding me that I was born to ruin her life. Constantly, constantly, would say even as a baby, "You were born to ruin my life. I don't want you. I didn't want you." Now keep in mind I wasn't her first child, I was her middle child. She loves my brother and my sister, her prince and princess, her pride and joy and everything... I was the one she just despised, I was the one she hated, she just didn't want anything to do with me.

'My parents would... when my parents would have horrible arguments, she would tell my dad she didn't want to be with him anymore. I remember this one time, this happened repeatedly but I remember this one time, this is just the memory I have where we're standing in the kitchen and my mom is standing by the sink and my brother on one side and my sister on the other side, and I'm standing next to my dad and she says: "I have my children. I don't want you and you can take that thing with you. I don't want that, I don't want it. Take it!" And my dad knew it, he always knew that that's what I was to her, was "it", a "thing", "that". She, uhm... she ridiculed me, humiliated me, beat me, caused my brother and my sister to do the same thing to me my whole life, and yet when I would scream and cry and fight back – I was the horrible child, the crazy one... and as a matter of fact and I'm sure it's because of the abuse, the story was that I didn't want to speak when I was little, when I was a child, when I was a toddler and I would sit in chairs and would just wring my hands over and over again. My mum swears that I did it to be evil, I did it to drive her crazy, that I just didn't want to talk; that I was, uhm... that that was a sign that I was crazy.'

(Margarita begins to cry and is distressed) 'And, uhm... I was born with really bad stomach problems, where I had to be constantly taken to the hospital from the time I was born because my body wouldn't digest food and I would get severely constipated, I was a newborn… and my mom to this day swears that even as a newborn… I would cry constantly at night, not from pain, not because I was sick, because my goal was to make her suffer. My goal was to make her lose sleep. My goal was to just hate her! That's all I ever did, from the time I was born was to make her suffer and miserable because… I was sick. Even as a newborn, before I could speak or anything.

'Now… My mother's abuse though is a cycle that has been repeated from her mother. My grandmother was a horribly abusive woman. The day she died I actually said, "Thank God!"

'We have a huge family; cousins, aunts, uncles, everything. Nothing! No contact with them.

'My grandmother did the exact same thing. My mom was me to my grandmother! The one that got treated the worst, the one that was hated the most, the one that was this and that, and that was repeated with me.

'My grandmother cheated on my grandfather constantly. And when my grandfather was away, she would bring men into the home and, uhm, some of these men would try to touch my mom and my aunts. So this whole family is just, uhm… a mess.

'My grandmother was also a compulsive liar.

'Uhm… just almost like, just, almost delusional… uhm, and my mom is the exact same way and the same thing that has happened with my family is what happened with my grandmother.

'Outside in the public eye, nobody would ever believe that my grandmother was capable of what she was doing because she was almost a saint and my family is like the exact same thing.

'In public people are like, "Oh my God what an amazing family! Perfect, great! Look at them so put together and this and that," but behind closed doors, a NIGHTMARE!

'So it's been hard for me to have people even believe what goes on in that home because they see one thing and of course it's the same story, over and over again.

'How could everyone in that family cover up something so horrible and only one person, you, claim that it's so bad?

'But that's my family, my family's like, "How embarrassing! We don't let the public to know what goes on in our home"… until it's me! Because I'm the outspoken one, because I'm the one that tries to bring light and embarrass the family. By bringing out the truth, they will bad mouth me, make me be, you know, crazy, a whore… I'm everything that they can make me out to be, just to protect themselves… and that's the cycle that, you know, keeps repeating itself.

'When I was in seventh grade, uhm, no I guess in sixth grade, my mother, you know, I went to school crying and I had marks on me and the school reported it to Protective Services and they went to the home… uhm of course like always, it was, "No, no it's Margarita, it's not the family, it's her." And Protective Services came back and said it's you! You're a troubled child and if we get a complaint from you, we're going to send you to "juvi".

'OK, seventh grade, my father gets arrested for beating me. I had a bruised lip and everything and, uhm, of course like always it was me! I asked for it, I was this, I was that.

'When we would go to therapy, my mother would grab me and tell me, "You'd better tell the therapist that everything is better. You better tell the therapist that things are good or I will beat you when we get home."'

'So instead of lying I would just stay quiet and I was angry and tell the therapist, "You don't understand." And she would say, "No, you're refusing to cooperate. No, you're just trying to be difficult."

'I would tell the therapist that it didn't matter and, "You don't understand. You just don't know, it doesn't matter and I'm not going to say anything." So then of course there you go, I am the problem one.

'You know I left when I was sixteen because I just couldn't handle my mum coming into my room in the middle of the night to beatings from her broom. Uhm, I got tired of it, I left and of course they told everybody that's proof. She's just always problems. She doesn't want to be in the home because she doesn't like rules and doesn't like anything. She just wants to be a whore to do this and that. Forget the fact that at sixteen I struggled to put a roof over my head, feed myself, try to finish school.

'I didn't get pregnant, I wasn't on drugs, I didn't do any of this stuff.

'I remember one of my aunts saying, "If my sixteen-year-old had left the home and doing what she's been able to do, I'd be proud of my daughter; she said she's not pregnant, she's not on drugs. She's still going to school, she's doing what she can. That says a lot about her." But no, they still try to portray me as a horrible person. So my mom? My mom contributed a lot; she was the source, the source of it all and, uhm, the theory is this: Why would my mom hate me and say I was born to ruin her life? How could a child be born to ruin your life unless the child holds something that's capable of ruining your life.

'What is a newborn capable of having except proof of an affair?

'… And just like my grandmother cheated, my aunts, not, uhm, especially my uncle, that they're not the children of my grandfather. Uhm, a lot of people have the same theory about me and my mum. And it's really funny that there's people who don't even know each other and have the same theory and when I ask them the name of the person I think is my real father, they all gave me the same name, which happens to be my father's brother, who happened to live with my parents at a certain point… and my mom always said that he was her best friend. He died when I was in fourth grade… and my mom… a week before he passed away my mom was losing her mind saying she kept hearing voices that something was wrong, something was happening and she kept hearing knockings and she kept hearing things and a week later my uncle-slash-father, supposedly – passed away.

'She was devastated, she was heartbroken, she cried, she said that she'd never forgive him for leaving without saying goodbye.

'And the funny thing is that my whole life my father said I was just like him... everything. My temper, my sense of humour, even being double jointed – that I was just like him, so I wonder if he knows or suspects or it's just pure coincidence that he's always compared me to him.

'... And my mom? We tell everyone that she was born in Mexico but she wasn't; she was actually born here in LA and my grandmother had her raised in Mexico.

'Funny thing about that story is that my mom and I always have Chinese people telling us, "Are you Chinese? Are you guys part Chinese? You know you must have some Chinese blood in you. You look mixed. You look Chinese."

'Funny thing about that is my mom was born in China Town.

'She was born in China Town and the fact that my mother got around... hmmmm, you know... makes sense.

'So you know, this whole thing about cheating and abuse and everything, these cycles just keep repeating themselves and just ruining lives, and I just keep falling into, you know, with my family – well, up until now. I needed to finally say, "I'm done!"

'I'm done. I'm done being the scapegoat. You guys can abuse each other but I'm not going to do it anymore and that is the source of the abuse with my father.

'My father would do anything my mum would ask. My father sides with her and he would abuse me to please her, to make her happy.

'I don't know why and I don't understand it. Uhm...' (she gives a long sigh) 'What else can I say? The abuse that I suffered from them or my father, I guess.

'Uhm... my mum once beat my hands with a belt so bad that she took the skin off my knuckles.

'I was six years old and she locked me in this old abandoned mobile home with bats in it because I wrote a little note on one of my notebooks saying "I love Mark"... this cute boy in class.

'My mom said that I was a whore, she knew I was a whore

and I would always be a whore, and she swore that she would take me to get checked to see if I was still a virgin.

'Uhm… my father used to, er, hook his belt and make it into a noose, hang it around my neck and lift me off the ground and beat me… and I couldn't breathe. I thought I was gonna die.

'I remember another time he punched me in the face so bad in third grade that he popped all the capillaries on the left side of my face, I had to go to school and tell everybody I fell off a swing and landed on my face… uhm, but it was constant, uhm, sticks, belts. My mom a few times tried to put my face in the flames of the stove.

'My dad used to beat me with the bungee cords you would use to hook things onto vehicles or trucks… uhm it was, it was horrible and it was unbearable.

'I started looking for love with men. I started looking for attention with men… at a really young age.

'I didn't lose my virginity until I was sixteen but, uhm, I started having inappropriate relationships with men when I was like in sixth grade, and we're talking twenty-something-year-old men.

'Uhm, when I was in high school there was thirty-something-year-old men, older men, and I'm assuming it must've been because of my father when I look back, you know.

'Older men wanting them to love me, to care for me, to treat me right,' (Margarita begins to cry) 'to respect me and… uhm… hmmmm… and it's, uhm… my life has been… you know, obviously it hasn't been a good life, having been out at sixteen, you're exposed to a lot of horrible things in life and that's exactly what's happened… uhm… bad places, bad situations, bad people.

'I've been raped several times… uhm, by people I trusted, strangers and the men that I have trusted: I had one boyfriend who tried to physically abuse me. His reasoning was, "You're used to it, why are you complaining about it? You know, you've dealt with abuse your whole life. Don't act like this is new to you, don't complain, you're used to it. What's the big deal? One more beating, one more person to beat you. What's the big deal?"

'Uhm… it's amazing what people think they can do to people just because of what's happened to them in the past.

'Uhm… my first boyfriend that I had at sixteen, uhm… I was the one that was really involved in school with anti-drugs, anti-drinking and driving… uhm, I was like the one everybody… I was the feminist, I was everything… probably 'cos of a lot of what happened to me in life.

'I was just strong and always, you know, always wanting to be the advocate, always wanting to speak out, and now it's funny, 'cos now even every time I've run into people from high school they say they pictured me being some hippie, travelling the world, protesting and, you know, fighting for people's rights and it breaks my heart 'cos that's exactly what I would've wanted to do had I been able to. Uhm… and I met this boy in high school and everybody was like, "What are you doing dating him, what are you doing dating him?" I couldn't understand why everybody was making such a big deal about this guy that I was dating, professors and everything and they were like, "No it's nothing, you just seem like an odd couple." This doesn't make sense but nobody ever told me anything.

'Started dating him a little after I turned sixteen, which was in March. I think I ran away from home in October or so… uhm… I was living with a girl that had graduated from my high school and, uhm, my ex-boyfriend, and I spent a lot of time with my ex-boyfriend. One day I'm in the car with him and he gets a phone call from his father saying, "Hey, uhm, you know, I need you!" and he says, "I can't she's with me," and he says, "Well I need you now, you're gonna have to bring her." Uhm… he took me with him and that's when I found out that both sides of his family were severely involved in drugs. His parents were divorced and his mother's side of the family, uhm… was huge and I mean when I'm speaking huge I mean cops, judges, detectives, everybody on the payroll… uhm, on the cocaine side of things and his father was weed… uhm, they

had everybody paid off and when I found out about it, I said this goes against everything I'm about. I can't be with you, I can't be in this and the family said the only way out for me is dead. So now I had to deal with abuse from him and his family. He became abusive and started beating me to the point where if I would go to school, nobody would recognise me… uhm… his family would stalk me. I would try getting restraining orders against him but they would always… the judge would approve the restraining order but of course when they would deliver it, something would always accidentally be wrong with it. If I tried to hide, they would assault my brother… uhm… I tried telling people and nobody… and everybody laughed because they said nobody could be that powerful, so it goes back to nobody believing me and so of course the only option I had, seeing nobody believed me and nobody would help me, is I kept going back to him to protect my brother and my family… And of course my family, everybody would say, "No, you went back there because you liked it. You went back there because you liked the beatings. You like this life," and this and that.

'It's like I was screwed if I did and I was screwed if I didn't; either way, nobody would ever understand; (she begins to cry) I put up with those beatings and I stayed there to protect my family, only to get no protection from them. I used to uhm… I tried three times so I could try to get away from him. I would try to leave him and, uhm, after my date would drop me home, they would be followed.

'They would have shotguns brought on them, telling them to stay away from me. It was bad. It was really bad. I think he finally left me alone when I was about nineteen or twenty, around there. Yeah… and this whole family, he could beat me in front of his whole family and his family would literally stand around and just laugh or complain how tired they were of my tears and crying and, you know, not listening to them and not, you know… if I just did things their way, I wouldn't be getting beat. I wouldn't be having these problems, you know – which is the same thing my family would say to me so, "If you will just do what we want, you'll be fine, you won't get abused. Keep your mouth shut and put up with it and cover it up like the rest of us do"… And again, I, you know, in the bad relationships I've had, I've noticed that, that attitude from men like it's like, you know… whatever I do to hurt you, just let it go. It's over, we're over it, big deal, move on instead of actually trying to see what happened, what went wrong, and I'm sorry and I'm not gonna do it again and you know let's fix it but it's just the way I am, it's the way I'm gonna be, just accept it. Just put up with it because if you don't, you're the bad girlfriend, you're the bad wife, you know you just can't let that go, you know you just wanna keep going at it.

'Why do you wanna figure it out, why you wanna talk about it? That's the way it is, that's how it's gonna be and let's just keep going. Because if you say something that's what causes the problem, not that I'm being abusive, not that I don't respect you; it's not any of that, it's you complaining…

'It's always, it's always me, because I complain about it, because I'm not OK with it, because I can't accept it – I'm the problem, not the fact that they're verbally abusive, not the fact that they don't respect me, not the fact that they cheat on me and just… it's me…

'Uhm… sexually abused… I suspect that I was sexually abused as a baby or as a toddler or something… uhm, nightmares I had, and that might be part of the reason why I spend so many nights crying… uhm but, uhm I guess because I was just… I knew about sexuality way too early and I must have been exposed to it.

'It was just a lot I know about sexuality and sexual feelings, uhm, you know, I just remember knowing about orgasms, even as a kid in elementary school and stuff like that and I always had conversations with grown women about sexuality and they would just kinda look at me, wondering how on earth I knew these things in fifth or sixth grade.

'They just, yeah… now when I look back I'm disturbed by it, uhm, so I'm almost 100% sure I was sexually abused as a child and obviously there was sexual abuse as an adult, and uhm, yeah… it caused me to be very promiscuous in life… uhm, I went through phases where I didn't care.

'I didn't care about myself, my self-respect, you know I had moments where I just said, "Why should I care, why should I care…" uhm… it never works out my way anyway. Uhm… so you know when people say you know you should've reported this to the authorities, why? Everybody turns on me! One way or the other, they turn on me and I don't get protected, I don't get what I feel I deserve as a victim or as a survivor.'

(She begins to cry) 'I don't get respect and I don't get protected and, uhm… and it's sad and this is why so many women do not report it.

'You know it's funny that I tell people; being raped is not what has destroyed me, I could handle the rape, I could handle getting through the physical part of what happened to me, what destroys me and what I believe destroys so many victims out there is not the actual incident… it's the way you get treated.

'The way family treat you, the way friends treat you, the way strangers treat you, the way authorities treat you… that will destroy you in a heartbeat and forever.

'The way nobody looks out for you, the way nobody believes you, the way everybody questions you, the way everybody judges you, the way everybody steps back and says, "Why! What did you do? It couldn't have been that bad. You must've done this, you must've done that"; or like my mom's famous words, "Why are you crying if you know you liked it?"… That is what destroys you.

'That is why some women make it, because the important people in their life know exactly how to protect and support them and others fall apart 'cos they have nothing and nobody. So it's not that we're liars and it's not that we like it, it's not that we enjoyed being there, it's that we get judged either way. You tell people about the abuse, nobody believes you, you stay in the abuse and people insist that you might like it. Leave the person who is abusive and oh well you're not forgiving, you're not tolerant. You know you're so quick to get rid of people you're not willing to give second chances. It's always the victim. Nobody goes to the abuser and says, "Get your shit together! Stop being an asshole, stop being an abuser. Stop doing what you do." NO! Everybody all of a sudden looks at the victim and goes, "You need to be God-like, you need to be Christian-like and you need to be…" They start bringing up religion and guilt tripping and who are you to judge and it's horrible.

'It's horrible. It's the victim's responsibility to fix everything and make everybody else feel better and fuck the victim! Screw our feelings, screw our experiences, screw our pain, screw us… it's sad. It's devastating… uhm, I haven't had a, I guess I haven't had a very serious relationship in a long time and part of that is that. I date people. I date people all the time and I don't want to make it sound like I've only had bad men in my life. I've had some really good men in my life.

'I tend to really like intelligent men. With intelligent men comes ambitious men and ambitious men are great at their careers and unfortunately those careers have had them relocate and them taken out of the country, across the country and, uhm, I'm just not one of those women, maybe I'll change, maybe I'll be like one of those women where I'm gonna get up and I'm gonna move my whole life for a man that I'm not married to. I'm not gonna live with a man I'm not married to.

'That's a big risk to take… uhm, so I've had some good men but life, you know, and careers, those things have sadly interfered with that. But along with that, I've also dated some horrible men and I'm the type of person, I see the first sign of a bad red flag and I'm done with them.

'I don't have high tolerance and it's funny because men always tell me, "Oh I love a strong woman who says what she thinks and she doesn't put up with things. Oh, she'll straighten me out," but the minute I start telling them that's not OK the way you speak to me, or it's not OK the way you treat other people… uhm, because for some reason men think that you could treat me like a princess but turn around and treat others horribly.

'Abuse is abuse, and just because you don't abuse me and you abuse others, I'm not OK with it and I won't be with you… uhm… and men are famous for saying, "But if I don't beat you and I don't cheat on you, they're just words," or "Those words aren't directed to you so what do you care?" And I have a tendency sometimes not to share the bad things with my friends because, you know, sometimes they're just too personal and sometimes I don't wanna share the things, I mean these men saying this to me or other people and I tell them, "Trust me, trust me, if I got rid of someone it's because I had good reason to."

'I'm picky, it's just that, you know, I just don't have tolerance for things so now, I have this reputation that you're always looking for a reason to get rid of people. No, it's just that we live in a society where nobody holds back anymore, we live in a society online, through text message, Instagram, Facebook, whatever it is, people feel really brave, people are big mouths, people are disrespectful, people you know and when we respond to it, we're horrible people. When we don't tolerate it, we break up with them, we're horrible people. Uhm… people just don't hold back, and a lot of my friends have been married for many years and they don't know what it's like to be out in this world these days dating.

'There's this one account and I always tell my friends, "Go on there!" I go, "Go on there!" 'cos I want you to see what it's like, what men are like when they get rejected. What men are like, you know, when they're told something they don't wanna hear. This is what I deal with in the dating world. You don't know what it's like to be dating now, it's a whole new world, it's a whole new attitude. They don't have the respect, they don't make men like they used to anymore, they really don't. And if you go on Instagram, go on "Tinder Nightmares". Uhm… Tinder is that dating app that you know, you go right, left, whatever but if you look up "Tinder Nightmares", the horrible things that men say to women and then you see the comments of what people may say, "Oh they're just words", or "Big deal".

The same thing repeating itself in this world. Uhm… you know, just over and over again, no matter what it is, women just have to be OK with it and put up with it. But if women have big mouths, if women say horrible things to men, we're these evil bitches, evil bitches… but boys are boys but women are evil bitches, always, always.

'Men can turn around and defend themselves, but when women do it, we're just evil, horrible bitches and it's sad, it really is.

'My mind is all over the place right now 'cos there's tons I could tell you and talk to you about. We could probably write books on my stories alone but, yeah… that's kind of the source of my abuse and the things I've gone through and the effects it's had on my life and uhm… and just, you know, I don't put up with it and I walk away in a heartbeat. I, you know, there's a Spanish saying, "Mejor sola que mal acompañada", meaning "You're better off alone than in bad company".

'And you know that's right. I'd rather be alone than in bad company, but because I'm alone, you know, people think you just, you're just looking for reasons not to be with someone. Not true! I would love to, you know, have someone that thinks the way I do, that looks out for other people, that cares for other people like I do and for each other. Emotionally? That seems impossible to find these days. Uhm… I hope I find it one day. I'm sure my red flags of intolerance levels kind of start flashing really quick before other people's would and that's because they don't understand the things I've seen. I see the patterns, I see the signs, I spot the things other people don't because of what I've been through and I try explaining that to them, and nobody will ever understand it without knowing how severe the life I've had is. So for now, I will leave you with this…'

Chapter 13
Benedetta's Story –
Messing With My Head...

'I am 46 and I am from Italy.

'I grew up with my paternal grandparents and my father, all living in the same house. My father and my mother separated when I was two as she was battling with severe depression, anorexia and anxiety.

'My dad had full custody of me as she attempted suicide several times.

'She died when I was ten years old. A jump from the third floor of a building, after numbing herself with alcohol and meds; she was too intelligent, too emotional, too fragile.

'If she had a thicker skin, she would probably still be here.

'I miss her every day and for years I have hated God and her for what happened, thinking it was my fault because maybe I wasn't a good daughter, but then I made peace with myself.

'After my mom's death, my dad made a solemn promise to dedicate himself to me until I was eighteen, then go to Africa (his real and endless love) to run his NGOs and other things.

'A year later, he was engaged. Two years later, he was remarried and within the next two years he had two other children.

'The promise made to me was broken and so was my heart.

'I chose to remain with my grandparents because my father was not willing nor able to have me around, so instead of letting me stay with his folks, he decided to send me to boarding school.

'I was missing that sense of validation and belonging from my father that any daughter deserves.

'No matter what I did, he was not happy. The course of studies I took, the music I would listen to, the friends I would hang out with… he always had something negative to say.

'With him it was and still is either his way or no way. He was not an abusive father as far as physical violence is concerned, but emotionally speaking he was so subtle and so good at making you feel like shit.

'He would never take any responsibility for his actions, it was always somebody else's fault, like his parents were to blame because of their intrusion in our relationship and it not being close when really it was about his "unkept" promises and couldn't see that was the issue with us, for me.

'He actually said he got remarried for ME yet I barely knew his wife!

'At 21, after graduating high school and spending a couple of useless years at the uni, I decided to start working and live by myself. He offered me a job in his company just so he could still keep an eye on me, control me and bring me down.

'I believe that this very poor relationship with my father has influenced quite negatively the choices I have made through the years, as far as love and partners are concerned.

'Even though people would describe me as a strong, direct, no-nonsense-taking person, always ready to help others even putting myself second, I have always felt this need of validation and belonging.

'That strong wish for a family that still is haunting me up until now.

'I've just always felt as if something was, is and will always be missing so I ended up with men very similar to him in character.

'I actually still struggle to accept that now my family ARE

my children and not my father and me, period.

'I ended up marrying a Nigerian man when I was 29, after just few months of dating, and no, I wasn't pregnant; I was just eager to finally have my own family.

'I guess I was in love with the idea of being in love, happy of having someone who was willing to be my family and to take care of me, but I was so naïve that I didn't realise that.

'I had only had one serious relationship with a guy from Albania before I got married, which lasted a few years, so I wasn't very experienced when it came to men.

'My husband was being pressured by his family to marry because he was getting old. He was just 32 but in his culture it was classed as old.

'His father didn't bless the marriage because he wanted his firstborn to have an Igbo wife which I clearly wasn't.

'I was a firm believer of the "love conquers all" shit and thought our love was enough but that wasn't the case.

'My father was also against this marriage to the point of my father doing background checks on my fiancé.

'My father demanded a church marriage and just wanted to control everything.

'He insisted on what he wanted in such a way that made me feel guilty, saying that I was not setting a good example towards my brother and sister and that being from a Catholic family, marrying in church was a must. Once again I submitted to his will to please him, even if he was not pleased anyway.

'The marriage did not start exactly the best way… the first night my husband was so drunk he couldn't even stay on his feet yet he still wanted to have our first time as a married couple.

'He forced himself on me, literally, and fell asleep snoring, totally shit-faced. This was just the beginning but within myself I was making excuses for him thinking he would change.

'And it changed, for the worse.

'He didn't appreciate anything I did. I remember one time he spat in my face telling me to, "Go and learn to be a wife!" because I didn't cook the food he wanted.

'I was on my knees crying, asking him, "Tell me how you want me to be a wife," but he couldn't answer. All I could do was to walk on eggshells and try to please him as much as I could.

'I fell pregnant with our son and because of all the stress, I ended up delivering my son two months early.

'He started controlling me financially and wouldn't even provide the bare necessities for the baby. I remember he took my car keys from me, saying that it was HIS car even though I paid for it with my own personal money and that I wasn't allowed to drive it. He eventually stopped paying the rent, paying the bills, saying that it was my family's duty to do so… he left the matrimonial home after he slapped and pushed me. All I did was ask for some money to get some medicine for the baby because he was sick. My husband got angry because I was insistent on needing the money. He said if I really wanted it I should prostitute myself for it… he never gave me the money.

'He put me through a ten-year court battle, ending in 2011 with the final divorce, obtained in his absence because in the meantime he'd left Italy and was nowhere to be found.

'After some few not-so-happy relationships, still searching for THE man who would love me and my child and validate me as an individual, I met my second husband in 2012.

'I was going through a very difficult time, still paying the consequences of my ex-husband's behaviour as he'd left tons of unpaid bills and stopped paying child support. I was facing eviction and I didn't want to get involved with anyone because I didn't feel it was right to put such a burden on another person.

'When I met Peter he seemed to be very serious about starting a family. He was 34, a bit younger than me, never married before, no children, no strings attached.

'He was living in a town not far from my city with his sister and her family sleeping on the couch, so when I explained my situation to him he offered to come to my help and share the expenses if we could live together.

'My son liked him and they got on pretty well. We both needed each other and we were in love – at least I was. He said he loved my confidence, my strong will, my being articulate.

'I thought he was the shy type, not knowing his very poor communication skills were a result of being a secondary school drop out! He could barely speak Italian, so anything official regarding him, I would take care of it and to be honest, I loved feeling useful and appreciated and treated like a queen because that's how he treated me at first.

'He even respected me to the point that, despite living together, we did not have sexual intercourse for the first three months of our relationship.

'The first time we slept together, I fell pregnant. I was shocked to say the least, especially after doctors told me in 2011 that I couldn't have children anymore.

'Everything seemed OK at first and we were a normal family. He was working, helping me with house chores, even being affectionate.

'Whenever he would go to his town to visit his relatives and his single friends, living large and thinking only about drinking and girls, his behaviour would drastically change.

'Even after one or two drinks he would become aggressive. He would keep in the house some vodka or gin.

'I saw red flags but I was ignoring them, thinking that with time, patience things would change. We had our son, also born two months early, and the day after his birth, my husband was laid off work.

'He didn't have the right paperwork to stay in Italy as he wasn't born there so instead of having to renew his papers every few months, we got married.

'In March 2014 we decided to come and live in the UK and that was the beginning of the downfall.

'I, as an Italian citizen, was my husband's sponsor, documents-wise and all of a sudden, that was now a big problem for him.

'He started being grouchy everyday, accusing me of being bossy, overbearing, of wanting to be the man of the house, just because he had to depend on me for the visa and all the other papers to move here.

'I came to the UK by myself for a week in April to sort out immigration stuff and found out when I got here that I was pregnant again; our first child together was only seven months old.

'This pregnancy was really unexpected, unplanned and kind of unwanted. My husband despite knowing that the "A" word wasn't in my dictionary, he told me, "GO AND REMOVE IT!!!"

'I refused because unplanned or not, this child was a gift from God.

'I left my husband in the UK by himself so he could get his papers in order and start working and I went back to Italy to sell all our belongings, pack a few and get ready to join him. I didn't know whilst I was away he had planned a "holiday" to meet one of his childhood friends, the "up to no good" type of friend no woman with a sound mind would want her husband to associate with. He went out every night getting drunk, meeting women and even setting up profiles on dating sites. Thinking that all this was absolutely normal, reinforced by his dear friend who was doing the same and blaming me as the cause of his stress which needed to be relieved in some way.

'At one point I did not want to leave Italy any more, I wanted to leave him in England by himself but then I thought about our kids, about all the sacrifices made for them to have a better future. In September, one day after our baby turned a year, I took a one-way flight with my two boys and came to join my husband here.

'The change of environment was shocking. I didn't like the UK, the system and being pregnant and with a toddler and a husband always working definitely did not help. I was lonely and unhappy and I had no support from my husband.

'He made me put all the money coming from my maternity pay from Italy to go into the family account, yet the money was never enough and I had to depend on him for everything. I hated that. Even though things were hard I felt I had to renew his sponsorship and to apply for his residency card.

'I remember an incident in November 2014, during a heated verbal altercation, after finding him AGAIN on a dating site, my teenage son broke in and, to defend me, he punched my husband who returned the punch. I was seven months pregnant, with heavy contractions. I called the police, and my husband got arrested and spent the night in jail, I and my sons spent the night in the hospital but we never pressed charges.

'My husband came home even angrier than before. The day I delivered our last son, in January 2015, he was in the theatre with me. He held my hand as I was crying, asking him: promise me everything is gonna be alright... he said yes. A few hours later, still inside the hospital, he was taking selfies. One of these pictures went straight on a dating site, where he was "looking for the love of his life".

'After I had my second son, I went through some post-natal depression.

'My husband would find all possible excuses to leave me home alone with the two little ones. The verbal abuse became heavier and heavier... I was ungrateful, I was a disgrace, I wasn't worth to be called wife, he would curse the day we married and on and on and on... up to telling me the kids I carried in my womb weren't his. He got removed from the family home twice in two months due to heavy altercations involving my teen son. He would upset me emotionally, covering me with all sorts of insults and it would get physical. Social services got involved and my kids were put under a child protection plan. He wasn't allowed to reside in the family home but we would see each other anyway.

'I was sick and tired of being humiliated yet I was determined to make this marriage work at all costs, I did not want my little ones to grow without a dad. I took him back in July 2015 after he begged me he had changed and wanted to make things work, but not once did the words "I'm sorry" come out of his mouth. Things went well for some months until something triggered the last straw; he used his last money to buy beer instead of nappies for the babies and I had the 'audacity' to complain about it. What a nagging wife, what an evil human being, the curses he threw at me, the insults, the humiliations. "Look at you, ugly, old and fat, nobody will ever want you with three kids, you will never find anyone as good as me because you don't deserve it… all you deserve is to be used and abused… all men will come close to you to use you and dump you because that's all you are worthy of. You can't even fuck, those women on dating sites are way much better than you, you are boring in bed. Your family wanted to get rid of you, that's why they wanted me to marry you, because you are useless." You are this and that and this and that. I couldn't take it anymore. I hit him and he threatened to slap me and bam, my teen son, who is a 6'2, 120kg rugby player, broke in again and the two started fighting. Police came AGAIN, he was arrested, given bail conditions and I had social services on my back again, accusing me of putting this marriage before my kids' welfare and threatening me that they would take them away. I believed that putting my marriage first was the right thing to do, especially for the kids.

'Receiving the court papers for care proceedings has been the wakeup call for me.

'My father was involved in the proceedings by social workers as a potential carer for the kids and when interviewed, instead of making things better, came to say I am a bad wife because of the upbringing HIS parents gave me.

'I couldn't risk losing my children forever by not putting a stop to the abuse and violence.

'At the first court appearance my husband manifested his "serious intention" of mending the marriage and to do whatever it took in his power to make it work, and have the kids remain with us and not go into care.

'I guess I wanted to believe him so I gave him the very last chance, knowing in my heart that he was doing it only for show.

'As part of the order, we attended the "Freedom Programme" which is a programme that deals with anger, violence etc. to stop men from behaving violently with their family and partners.

'We had two counselling sessions and on the last one, he still blamed everybody and their mama for all that happened, never took responsibility and started blaming me again. That night I left the session and I decided enough was enough.

'Without any second thought, I informed our court social worker I wanted to officially separate and that I would eventually seek for divorce. It was a very risky move to separate during care proceedings but I did what I had to do for the welfare of my kids and myself.

'The care proceedings ended positively in August; the kids are home with me. They see their dad every week and as far as him being good with them, I can't say anything. My husband continues to attack me from time to time by text but I ignore him as much as I can. I am about to start the divorce petition, even if it is not what I wanted.

'God will eventually take care of everything. The relationship with him has left big scars, on which I am working on.

'It's left me drained in my spirit and in my physical strength. Dealing with an abusive person who is in denial is really energy consuming. I have put on 30kgs in less than a year due to comfort eating, ended up with sleep problems as well.

'I have always been a plus-size woman, happy and confident of my body but after being abused, despite knowing that all the crap my exes told me was not true, I am kind of disliking myself, seeing me old and not pretty yet unable to get out the loop to diet and take proper care of myself.

'For months I had a lot of anger within me and a lot of doubts as well, because no matter how strong you are, when you are constantly brought down, you start to believe it is your fault, that maybe he is right in saying all he says and your mind starts whirlwinding until you are not able to think anymore.

'I am due to re-start some CBT sessions, interrupted because of some physical health issues. Despite all this, I am still positive, I continue seeing good in people and doing good to people no matter what. I want to conclude my story with one of my favourite Bible quotes: "'For I know the plans I have for you,' declares the LORD, 'plans to prosper you and not to harm you, plans to give you hope and a future.'" This is what I believe and I pray for my children and myself.'

Chapter 14
Phoenix's Story – Still I Rise...

'My name is Phoenix and I'm 54. I'm from Ghana.

'Looking back, I think my parents' marriage was the first major influence in my choice of a partner, and the behaviour that I assumed when I actually got married.

'My mother was a very strong character, extremely strong and very forthright. She was very focused, very determined; she knew her own mind and my father was the opposite.

'He was very passive and very calm, and he was happy for her to take the lead in I think a lot of the life decisions that they had to make.

'When I was younger my parents lived apart. My father lived in another European country than we did and only came home at the weekends, and I remember from very early on that my mother seemed to always be very irritated by my father's laissez-faire attitude towards things.

'There were lots of shouting matches, I mean I shouldn't say shouting matches – when she got angry, my father wouldn't say anything and she would eventually run out of steam and things would go on as before... uhm... we moved to Ghana when my parent's marriage broke up... uhm... my mother initiated the divorce and in revolt, I remember I went and lived with my father, and I think the seeds of how a marriage should be got planted in me then.

'Erm… fast forward to when I actually got married to someone who was my high school sweetheart, in the sense that we wrote romantic letters to each other, there was no physical relationship; this happened after we got married and I think my first caution to anybody would be before you get married to anyone you need to live with them, or you need to date them… for a long time to see them in every possible scenario and see how they handle themselves. Because looking back, if I had… if we had dated longer, I think I would have run away. There's no way I would have put myself in that situation.

'Alright, to help you understand my situation: I had a child before I got married - this was way, way back in the 1980s and having a child out of wedlock was seen as a bit of a disgrace, so, erm… I always had that stigma, especially since I didn't get married to the child's father there was that stigma that I was a 'born one' as many people very crudely put it… and I think when I met this person, because he was someone who I had communicated with for a long time, I thought I knew him.

'What I didn't realise was when you are having a written relationship with someone, you always put your best, the best part of you out there, you don't put out the real you.

'So when he met me I had a good job, was doing well and he couldn't get enough of me, you know… and I was flattered by it and I think there was also, deep inside me, because of his profession, being married to him would accord me the respectability I had lost by having a child out of wedlock, and I would be a "Mrs.", a Mrs. married to this person who had a good profession and you know, it would restore my dignity, my status. Very, very stupid but those were the times in which we were in.

'The marriage started off well enough.

'I remember the first day that he hit me.

'I remember my first reaction when he hit me. I thought, "Oh my God!" You actually see stars when somebody hits you that hard and it was over something so nonsensical. I can't even believe it, and I should have left then, and when you are so desperate to hold a marriage together, and I forgot to add that because of my parents' divorce, I felt there was this pressure on me to prove to everyone that I could do it, that I could keep my marriage together... and because my mother was the one who had instigated the divorce, there was this stigma that I was the daughter of the woman who divorced her husband so I was carrying so many burdens on me.

'To give the background to the first... beating, a friend of his came to visit, someone he hadn't seen for a long time. So as is customary, we gave him a meal and, erm... I was standing on the balcony with a friend who'd come to visit me.

'So I kept an eye on my ex and his friend who were chatting, so when I realised he had finished eating, I went in and asked him if he'd finished the food and you know, I took... I cleared his plate away, so when he was leaving he was really happy and this was my first time of meeting him and he said, "Thank you so much, I've had a lovely time," and all that and he went away, promising to come back and see us again with his wife.

'A short time after that my friend said goodbye and left as well.

'I remember my ex had been drinking. Suddenly he stood in front of me and he said, "How dare you disgrace me like that, how dare you clear away, how dare you do that?"

'I remember I was stunned and wondering what I had done and he said, "How dare you take the plate when he hadn't finished eating? Why are you disgracing me?" You know, very, very aggressively and I was in a panic and I said, "I didn't do that, I asked him if he was finished"... and then he slapped me, so hard... but then it wasn't the pain of the slap, it was the shock, you know, I can't explain it. I saw stars and the sad thing, the saddest thing, and then he said, "Tell the truth, I need you to tell the truth"... and he slapped me again, and I said, "I'm telling you the truth, I didn't clear it away until he'd finished eating. Why would I do that?"

'I think he slapped me a third time and I didn't even run away, I didn't even hit back, I was just so stunned and then I started crying after that and then he went away and he ordered me not to leave the house because I'd got a bump on my forehead and he said I wasn't allowed to leave the house. He travelled to go and see his family in a different town. We were going to make the trip together but I was a mess so I didn't go and it's so, it's just... I just can't understand why I made him make me believe I'd done something wrong.

'I kept replaying it in my mind and I thought, maybe the man hadn't finished... I couldn't remember! And you know, because he was so forthright, he made me accept to myself that I'd done something wrong when I hadn't.

'I was so ashamed, I couldn't tell anybody.

'I couldn't tell my dad about it, didn't tell my parents about it, erm... I mentioned it to my brother-in-law, who was furious and had wanted to come and speak to him about it and I said, "No! If you come and speak to him he's gonna be more angry with me". That's the sad part... looking back I can see I was just that desperate for us - to stay married to him at all costs. This was my respectability, this was my dignity that I allowed him to brainwash me into thinking I'd done something wrong.

'Many, many years later, I confided in this friend who had visited me at the time and she was horrified, and she said, "NO! I remember you asking the man if he'd finished eating and him joking and saying there's nothing left on the plate and saying it was really delicious and complimenting me about the food... so that was the first time, and I think actually the only thing I can say is that don't allow a second time. You need to get out, you need to go."

'So he came back from his trip, apologetic, crying and I remember this thing that he said that, "Why did you make me do that, why did you make me do that to you?" and so that... he put the blame on me! That I had made him do what he did and that was the beginning of this hole that got deeper and deeper every day, and I found myself shackled in this existence of abuse and physical abuse and mental abuse and emotional abuse and financial abuse that didn't end, or continued for the next twenty-two years.

'When a man hits you... you don't stay. You don't make any excuses. You leave him. Because when a man hits you once, he WILL hit you again and it will NEVER end, until you leave him.

'After that first incident, erm... looking back I can see that, that's when he decided to, I don't even know what he decided... he decided to take control of me, body, soul and spirit. So he started by isolating me from my family.

'My brother came to visit: he accused my brother of stealing my daughter's bicycle and then whenever I spoke to my mum, he would accuse me of gossiping about him, and when my sister came there was always something, some drama about it.

'Little by little he, erm... isolated me from my friends. I remember a friend coming to visit and, erm... him saying afterwards that my friend was trying to arrange for me to go and meet another man. It was like every time there was someone close to me, he created a scenario where that person was a threat to our marriage or that person was complicit in me doing something wrong. And then there was this insane jealousy of me having a relationship with any man. I'm talking about platonic relationships and, erm, apart from that initial incident there was an instance where he, he hit me.

'What aggravated it, what made it more stressful was that for the first five years of our marriage I suffered about eight miscarriages and I believe a lot of the miscarriages were brought on by stress.

'And then I changed jobs and was working at a... by the way I need to say that I wasn't an illiterate; I was highly educated, had my own profession and everything.

'So I changed jobs and started working for someone who had a reputation as a bit of a womaniser (I was married at the time) and part of the perks of the job is that we were given, erm... cars to use, official cars to use... you know, in a personal capacity and I remember bringing the cars home and him... erm... it was a nicer car than the one that he used and he used a car as well. And I remember him coming home one weekend after taking the car for a wash and him telling me he had taken the car to... erm, a car wash for it to be washed and that the attendant who washed the car, said to him that, "Oh the man who owns this car, he only gives it to his girlfriends to use so the person who's using this car is the man's girlfriend"... I mean something so ludicrous!

'And so he came home and said this is what the attendant said and I said, "Well that's ridiculous," because the owner of the... my boss wasn't even the person who allocated the vehicles.

So about a year or so later, I was made redundant from my job so had to look for another job.

'My husband woke me up in the middle of the night and said I needed to confess that I had been sleeping with my boss and that this was the reason why I had been made redundant - and I said nothing of the sort had ever happened. My boss had never propositioned me... and HE BEAT ME!... HE BEAT ME! He slapped me, he punched me. He was a tall heavy-set man. He beat me as if he was beating his own child. HE BEAT ME... And a neighbour who lived in the next house shouted to ask what was happening. HE BEAT ME!... and whilst he was beating me he said that I needed to confess and that he wouldn't stop beating me until I confessed that the man was my boyfriend, I was having an affair with the man, but I said I cannot confess to something that has not happened.

'HE BEAT ME.

'And while he was beating me I wanted to get up and use the washroom, he escorted me to the washroom, kept the door open whilst I used the washroom and when I got up, he resumed beating me. The only time he stopped beating me... we had a house-help and she came and shouted at him and she was crying and told him to stop; he refused.

'The only reason why, the only point at which he stopped was when our next door neighbour who was a retired soldier shouted and said that he was going to bring a gun round if he didn't leave me alone.

'And so... and then I stayed, you know.

'I stayed, battered and bruised, but I still stayed.

'And the following day, as was the norm, he said I'm sorry, he cried... erm, brought me things to... I can't even remember what shit he brought me and at that time I was so worn down. I was ashamed, everyone in the vicinity had heard him beating me. I couldn't got to work for a couple of days 'cos my face, there were contusions on my face, but the sad thing was that I stayed... and I stayed because he had eroded my self-worth, he had eroded, you know, distanced me from my family, and he had put me in this incredible state of mind that my marriage was still the only thing that mattered and I was still blaming myself that if I tried hard enough, or if I did... I didn't even know what I was thinking. But then I stayed...

'And I had my pregnancy; during the pregnancy he was quite supportive, then after my son was born and I was breastfeeding my son, he said I was getting sexual pleasure from breastfeeding my son. And so insisted that I stopped breastfeeding my son and then one day in the middle of the night when my son woke up, and you know, he was trying to stop the breastfeeding, he would sit beside me whilst I was breastfeeding my son. It was like being, I don't even know what situation to describe as being in.

'I remember even soon after my son was born, my mother came to stay. He was so incensed at the fact that my mother came to stay that he threatened to take my child away and threatened that I would never see the child again... and yet I stayed...

'The early stages whilst my son was a baby, he would come home drunk and accuse me of having every, any man he knew, I ever knew, was the father of this child.

'It was manic... I was an emotional wreck and yet... I stayed. I stayed because I thought, "I've got my family now. I've got a girl and a boy and I have a husband and I've got the prestige of being, erm... married to somebody in this profession"... and the saddest thing was people from the outside envied me so much because they felt I had this magical life.

'There were times where he would beat me and be in the middle of slapping me or doing something and someone would pop by and he would stop, and he would put on this fantastic attitude of, "Hello darling," and you know calling me darling and everybody envied me 'cos they thought I had this most amazing marriage, and there was a day that he went out drinking and he was so paranoid when we went out with friends. Even with close friends, he would accuse me of flirting with them so I couldn't make eye contact with anybody.

'As soon as we got home, if there was anybody who I'd known before I met him, as soon as we got home it would be interrogation time. And there was one night where he went out drinking and came home and once again demanded that I confess that I was sleeping with my ex-boss. Somebody who had never even propositioned me before, and that if I didn't confess, he would kill me.

'So that was the only day I really feared for my life and I kicked him in the groin, I took my child and I left home and I went to go and stay with a friend. So that was the point at which I had to tell my mum about what was happening.

'My mum came down and there was like a family meeting and he had to... he was asked to explain why he had touched me and he couldn't explain it.

'That was the last time he actually touched me.

'But then before then, it's a bit of a blur now, he would beat me. He would beat me so much I would have contusions on my leg, and I'm a black woman and I would have black and red bruises on my thighs... and sometimes I would have to run away to a friend's house in the middle of the night... (Phoenix exhales deeply and sighs.)

'For some time, things settled down a bit and we had another child and we decided to relocate to the UK and I was so happy because I thought at least we're gonna be away from, you know, all the stresses and whatever in Ghana and move over here, but the madness continued.

'At this point I was isolated from everyone. I couldn't speak to my mum openly; I had to call my mum when he wasn't around.

'My father had died, my younger brother was resident... was taking different overseas jobs because of his job and my sister ostracised, isolated her as well.

'We moved here and I thought this was going to be a new beginning, things would change... but things didn't change.

'And even here, the abuse... the mental, there was no physical abuse but there was emotional abuse and there was verbal abuse.

'He would come back and tell me to go and look in the mirror and ask myself whether I thought I was beautiful.

'Then he would say, "You're not beautiful. I knew you weren't beautiful when I married you. I thought you were sensible but since I married you, I've found out that you're stupid as well. You're the ugliest woman I've ever seen."

'We were married but he would not provide for the children. He would argue with me over child benefit payments because he couldn't understand why I wasn't giving them to him.

'I would come home from work and I wouldn't want to go home. I would drive to a supermarket car park, then I'd sit there and call my mum and have a conversation with her; and each day you'd come home with your heart in your mouth because you wouldn't know what kind of mood he would be in.

'I tried to do my Masters when I was in Ghana and I took study leave from my regular employment; it was unpaid study leave.

'This was at his encouragement 'cos he'd said that he would sponsor me to do my Masters, and I remember being reduced to almost destitution because the money that he would give me for me to commute to the university campus and back was just enough for that.

'I had no money to do anything else and it was such a horrendous time for me, and even though I was doing my

Masters because most of the classes were in the evening, I would come home to a barrage of abuse and accusations that I had been sleeping with my lecturers and it was… I can't, I can't even explain how terrible it was; and it got so bad that I just abandoned the idea of continuing my Masters as I just couldn't cope with the mental stress, the physical stress, the commute and the emotional stress – I just couldn't cope! So I had to abandon that.

'He would beat me as if he was beating his fellow – somebody of his own stature.

'He would beat me… and I would see stars… and yet I stayed.

'And I think when you're in that situation, you're ground down to a point where you have no self-respect, where you have nothing, only thing, I can't even explain it on holding together this shambles of a marriage, of an existence, and still holding on to the hope that you can make it work.

'I have two sons, and I think my greatest fear was that they would follow, they would emulate their father's behaviour regarding the verbal abuse, the physical… and I remember my elder son saying to me, such poignant words, he said, "Mum, the day you get the courage to divorce this man, your only regret will be for not having done it sooner"… and I looked at my child and wept, and I still didn't have the courage to do it.

'And he was out having affairs. I knew about them and I was even happy, because it meant that I didn't have to have much of a physical relationship with him and I think I just kept thinking in time things would just sort themselves out. And I think I kept consoling myself that at least he's not beating me and that the verbal and mental and emotional abuse was something I could cope with.

'Things sort of kept on like that till the final straw that broke the camel's back was about four years ago, when he seized my car keys and tried to sell my family home from over my head… under one pretext or the other, and I got legal advice about that and got the police involved and he was asked to leave… and that's what set me free.

'There's so much, I can't even. There's so much I just realised I forcibly erased them from my mind but the lessons that I have learnt are this:

'When a man touches you, you leave him.

'There are no excuses.

'There are no explanations.

'When a man touches you, he's abusing you, he's hurting you, and that is not love.

'Marriage means nothing.

'Marriage is not, and should not be seen as an emblem of respectability.

'You should be respectful of who you are as an individual and you should only marry someone because you love them and not because the marriage will afford you any kind of respectability; and being in a relationship with someone who treats you in such an inhumane manner, is not marriage, it is servitude... it is slavery.

'We need to teach our children to be respectful of each other. We need to teach our girls to say, "NO!"

'We need to teach them to get the education they need and teach them to stand on their own two feet.

'We need to forget about society's idea of marriage making a woman or making a person or making them more important and we need to... and I don't even have the words to say it but I'll get back to it again.'

(Phoenix stops speaking as she is too upset to continue.

She come back to complete her story after a few days...)

'Uhm... my mother-in-law, I believe was, erm, was a lot to blame for my husband's temperament and for his, erm, siblings' temperaments because I realised that there were four brothers and they all had this very dismissive, abusive attitude towards their spouses and I suspected strongly that my father-in-law had probably adopted the same kind of an attitude towards their mother, which is why all of them thought it appropriate to disrespect their spouses and I know in one other case that he also physically abused his wife, and with the other he attempted to do so but the lady did not permit him to take those liberties with her - and it also comes back to, er... age-old belief that a male child was superior to a female child, therefore was allowed to disrespect them. And I strongly believe that my father-in-law must not have treated my mother-in-law with a lot of respect and maybe because of her level of education or her upbringing, she thought it appropriate to instil in her sons a sense that they were superior beings and there were instances where she was privy to the fact that her son had maltreated or abused me because she was with us at the time and she turned a blind eye, a complete blind eye and so she was as it were, erm... how do I even say it? She wasn't openly calling and saying, "What on earth are you doing? Stop it!" or anything of the sort, she was just... it was, to her, it was a normal part of how a marriage should be and there was a point in time I think I realised if I did not get rid of this man, I was providing a blueprint for my sons and letting them know that it was l alright for them to disrespect their girlfriends and their wives and that for my daughter, it was alright for her to be accepting of such behaviour...' (Phoenix sighs deeply; most of her testimony has been with a faltering voice and surprise at some of what she is revealing. She's found the experience really tough but cathartic – grateful for being able to tell her story uninterrupted and without judgement)

Chapter 15
Reflections...

Breathe.

Exhale.

Close your eyes and bring yourself back to the here and now, the place where you have control and the final say in what happens in your life.

Maybe you've read some of these stories and they resonate with you on some level, or maybe you're living the life of Malia, Margarita, Bernadetta or Phoenix. I know those stories may have been hard to read but I hope we can look at what these women have shared and let it empower us to begin to lay the foundations to rewrite our own stories where we need to.

Let's explore some of the issues that they touched on and see where we can identify the red flags, add to our knowledge of not only predatory behaviour, but the effects on children being raised in a home or environment where fathers are either absent and taking no interest in their children, or present but passive and ineffective in their protection and upbringing.

From the very beginning I spoke quite clearly on the pictures we paint for our children and the importance of our fathers validating, supporting and showing us what positive and safe strength looks like, to help us shape our choices in the partners we end up with. The importance of a father's validation to help us avoid the need for men to take on that role, because let's face it: it's rarely ever done without coming at a very high price.

The mothers in these equations are of paramount importance. Remember I said the mother is the one we often emulate or draw from, to decide who we are and how we 'allow' ourselves to function in the relationship.

Malia

Malia's story brings to light a number of issues to me, but different things will resonate with each reader dependent on the experiences you've had.

The first thing that jumped out to me was the lack of protection her mother offered to her and her siblings. Because of the method by which Malia and her brothers ended up in America, her mother was immediately placed in a vulnerable and compromising position.

Being totally reliant, with small children, on a partner who was not the father of her children for food and shelter was always going to be a needless risk.

She was not responsive to the children's cries for help, even after a disclosure of the abuse was made.

Malia's mother's behaviour is sadly not unique. Many women choose not to act upon the disclosures made by their child about abuse. There are many reasons for this, ranging from not wanting to lose the man they've chosen to be with, fear of leaving, fear of being alone, choosing not to believe their child as well as others.

Sometimes it's hard to accept that a mother can actually choose an abusive partner over her children, but this happens time and time again.

It would be difficult to find out why Malia's mother made the choice to remain with the abuser of her children for the time that she did; in the absence of speaking to her, to understand why she made the decision to bring her children into a situation she must have known could be detrimental to her and her children if it didn't work out.

When we look at the painting of pictures for our children I mentioned in the very beginning, the picture painted in this home is one where the message is that nobody is there to protect you. Fathers are too weak to ensure you won't be taken away in the dead of the night and any male that comes on the scene as a provider or protector comes at a cost, demanding in return what no child – or anyone for that matter – should ever have to pay.

Malia's childhood experiences formed mistrust, not just of men but of people as a whole. This has marred Malia's view of the world and how she is to function within it effectively.

She has however acted the opposite to her mother by being the protector of her own children and ensuring no harm came to them, but being overly protective and suspicious of partners eventually led to the demise of her marriage.

It's not unusual for an abused child to go completely the opposite way to how they were raised once they have their own family but within that, there are often a number of varying issues that the parent may feel and struggle with. Without help to deal with what essentially is childhood trauma, it can stifle or hamper any healing that should be experienced. Even with the necessary support from professionals such as counsellors etc. it's still a long hard road to recovery but it's not impossible.

Protecting our children must be our number one priority for any mother. Prioritising the welfare of our children must trump any other obligation in our lives. It must supersede by millions of miles the choice to be with a partner or anything remotely similar. If we fail, we set our children up to fail. The failure of a mother to listen and believe her children when they have taken the brave step to find a voice they have probably been told to never use, deserves to be heard. Too many children are silenced, laying the foundation for a troubled life.

Malia should be proud of herself. She has fought and won all her life from what I have come to learn of her life and experiences.

She tried to find a way out when nobody else would help her. I don't know many kids that would try to poison their abuser to set themselves free at that age, but she did. Of course I'm not sending a message to say take the law into your own hands, but when the law doesn't know you exist, I would be the last to tell a child being sexually, mentally and physically abused not to protect themselves if they could. The sad thing for me is that a child should never ever be in that position in the first place.

Malia leaving home to escape the horrors there and entering into abusive and damaging relationships is another common action that follows living in an abusive or emotionally unstable home.

It's important to try and recognise the forming patterns when you've suffered childhood abuse, and see where history may be repeating itself or where you may be exhibiting behaviours that may be destructive or abusive.

Do you date abusive men?

Are you often angry, depressed, anxious?

Are you abusive?

Do you fall into abusive platonic relationships?

Do you have issues with drugs and alcohol?

Do you experience recurring nightmares?

Some of the above are a few manifestations in behaviour that can be explored to try and trace its roots. A lot of things we do to attain healing and peace of mind is exploratory, so these questions can be used as a starting point to finding answers to explain why we act in certain ways, often without realizing it.

Malia being able to speak about her experiences was a huge step in the healing process and has set her up to want to be able to live a normal life.

So many devastating things have ocurred in her life, but and she knows though these awful things happened to her - they are not her.

The constant battle to find inner peace and happiness and the ability to change her perception or paradigm of her experiences, is something only she can do. With the right support, she will be able to realise that dream of happiness.

The one thing that can never be taken away from Malia is the fact that she survived. There is no arguing of the fact that she had been 'saved' twice. The horrible experience of rape at gunpoint, and the attempted suicide that followed, still didn't manage to succeed in taking her life. Yes she has a battle and a long road ahead but she still has a chance to change the end of her story. There are so many others who don't make it, whether it's because they have just lost the fight within or the fact that someone has taken the fight from of them.

There is a reason for everything and yes, it's mighty hard to understand the reason for someone to go through such repeated pain, but I truly believe there is one.

It's not always possible to have the answers to hand, but eventually things have a way of making sense and the reason those experiences happened become clearer in time.

In simple terms: is the glass empty or half full? Is there even a glass in the first place?

My desire would be for Malia, and every woman who has had their emotional, sexual or mental boundaries violated, to be able to come to a place where control is back in their hands. It takes a heck of a lot to get to the mountain top, but where there is life there is hope and if the desire to win is there, then you'll win.

I believe Malia will be able to live life as she wants to with the help and support that she's willing to accept.

Margarita

Margarita's mother appears to be the weapon that acted as the source for an immense amount of pain and suffering Margarita experienced as a child.

Margarita's mother, having experienced similar treatment by her own mother, didn't stop her from allowing history repeating itself.

Margarita was totally rejected by her mother and there was nothing to go on in terms of there being any reference points one could identify to show any motherly love or concern from her mother, even when she was a sick baby and little child.

The rejection was very deliberate and constant; because of this, Margarita knew exactly where she stood with her mother, so as painful as it has been for her, her expectations were managed and she knew there was nothing she could do to be accepted or loved by her.

Her father on the other hand showed some semblance of wanting to be a father to Margarita, but looking at the dynamics of his relationship with her mother, he felt that he was not able to express his love for his child.

It's interesting to see that though the abuse was predominantly perpetrated by her mother, the effects of her father's failure to protect and defend her has had a significant impact on how Margarita views men, relationships and fatherhood.

Margarita identified herself that she had been acting out the effects of her poor and now non-existent relationship with her father in the relationships with men when she was a young girl.

Her wanting a father-figure and not having one in the father that she knew meant that from very early on, she sought to reenact that relationship. Once older, the expectation to be betrayed and let down was a pattern she wasn't aware she had formed until she reflected on the effects of her experience with her family during the telling of her story.

Margarita held her father, not her mother, to greater account and responsibility to have taken care of her.

At every given juncture where her father should have stepped up and been a father, he failed and Margarita strongly believed that the course of her life could have taken a very different turn if he hadn't.

Margarita's story really demonstrates the profound effect of having a father who is present, but absent emotionally.

The damage of his passivity became more devastating when this acted as an enabler of the emotional abuse, until he began to assist in the physical abuse as well.

The revelation of her paternity being called into question is another element of instability that she has had to deal with.

Every child wants to know where they come from and this

is heightened when that child is being neglected or facing other forms of abuse. Margarita wanting to know if her father was indeed her uncle acted as a type of escapism from the reality – his untimely death had a profound effect on her.

The idea of having a knight in shining armour out there somewhere, who could possibly take her away from all her pain, seems to have acted as a mental and emotional escape from the reality of who her father really was – the reliance on the off chance of her 'real' dad stepping up and claiming her.

Margarita's mother and father's rejection and abuse have made her very determined not to allow herself to fall into abusive relationships now that she is older. We did explore that victims of abuse can either be very determined to ensure they are never victimised again, or they can relive the abuse they have suffered in the past in future relationships.

Margarita mentions possibly being a victim of child sexual abuse but isn't sure.

Many people may not understand how powerful the mind is in trying to protect itself from profoundly traumatic memories.

It is actually not unusual at all for victims of child abuse or other traumas to have a complete memory loss of the said trauma.

What Margarita describes has been researched by psychologists, confirming this is not a unique phenomenon.

The effects of such experiences, though not present in the conscious mind, are still able to manifest in the physical in various forms such as anxiety, mental illness, depression, drug and substance abuse as well as other visible effects.

Trauma shows up in different ways to different people and at different times during their life's journey. The triggers that bring the hidden memory into the present can be anything.

Going back to Malia's story, she too could not recall her real dad, having been removed from his care and brought to America. She suffered nightmares for a number of years before being able to piece her memories together and come to the conclusion that the person who had been sexually and physically abusing her was not her real father.

The mind has its way of working in this manner as a coping mechanism. It is the mind's method to try to remain sane and functional the best it can under the circumstances in which it's required.

This is really a crucial area to take note of for a very important reason: when victims of rape and abuse fail to disclose their abuse, it's not because they are fabricating stories.

The memory loss isn't intentional or done to deceive, but rather an unconscious and involuntary action. It is therefore imperative that when a victim of abuse does disclose an experience – that they have formerly denied even – that we are gentle in bringing them to a place where they feel they can recount their ordeal and we need to assist in providing the necessary psychological support they require by being sensitive to their challenges in trying to recall an event or set of events that have been buried for a period of time.

We must be careful not to be quick to dismiss people who reveal their trauma and abuse in this way but rather seek help to get them in the right environment for support.

Benedetta

Benedetta's story is classic of the woman that is looking for love and validation because her father has failed to provide it.

The lack of validation and broken promises is a catalyst for creating that insatiable desire for a woman or girl to seek love and acceptance from her relationships: Benedetta was no different.

When Benedetta lost her mother at the tender age of ten, it would have felt like abandonment. To have to deal with grief under such horrific circumstances must have been incredibly difficult for her.

The place of the mother in the life of any child is important and leaving by 'choice' through suicide can be interpreted by a child as feeling they weren't worth sticking around for.

It's so hard for a young mind to rationalise why their mother would leave them in this way.

The emotions we go through when a loved one dies are so intense, and for children it's no different. Maybe it's even more difficult for young minds to grasp the concept and finality of death than it is for an adult. Adults have seen a level of real life that children generally wouldn't have seen and are therefore less likely to have the emotional capacity to easily manage the process of bereavement. It would be, in my opinion, even more important to pay particular attention to a child who has lost someone as close as their mother.

From Benedetta's story, she seemingly received this love and support from her father, but not for long. Her father's failure to keep his promise was like a second abandonment because he didn't keep his promise to look out for her and put her first. His moving on so quickly and creating a new family was an outward demonstration of what was being replaced, with the promise her father had made, with a new wife and family. He moved on very quickly with no real sense of emotional responsibility to his young daughter.

When a father makes a vow to his little girl, she expects him to keep it. If he doesn't she's likely to develop a suspicion of men in her relationships as well as a feeling of unworthiness when promises are made after all, if your own father can't keep his word under such dire circumstances, why would anyone else?

Benedetta's desire to look for love and validation is rooted in her childhood experience and perception of her father and how he related to her.

Falling into abusive relationships, looking for approval from the men that were abusing her and taking them back, after varying forms of abuse from coercive control to physical and financial abuse, is characteristic of a woman who had the childhood background and circumstances she had experienced.

When a man decides to strip you of your self-respect by playing with your mind, throwing endless insults and put-downs, it will begin to have an effect on you.

With each curse word hurled at you, every threat, every word spoken in anger, every calm and calculated promise of pain communicated through gritted teeth, it begins to wear you down and break you emotionally and mentally until you begin to doubt the very essence of who you are. You're made to question the very basics of every decision you make, not trusting yourself to think independently anymore.

You know you need to leave but can't and you keep saying to yourself he'll change but never does - this was Benedetta.

If we can retrace our steps to the place of that little girl, if we can go there and demand the answers from ourselves, then we can attempt to draw parallels to see where the emotional and mental potholes of our past might be hiding and present them to our future and current selves to deal with in the here and now to heal.

If we can get help to identify the limiting beliefs that take residence in our heads, we will be on our way to freedom from the issues that take hold of us due to what we've experienced in past abusive liaisons.

Benedetta finally found the strength to say 'No'. No to being exploited, being emotionally and mentally abused and having herself subjected to financial deprivation for the sake of keeping her marriage.

It is worth mentioning that Benedetta's need to be needed, i.e. taking on the role of the 'rescuer' in her relationships, forms part of the patterns I have mentioned earlier. The man will shy away from responsibility if you present yourself as his saviour. When you have men who are insecure, they often will turn to exert their authority and validation at your expense; this was experienced by Benedetta too.

It's clear in hindsight how much some of us will sacrifice to remain in a relationship. In this case there were children witnessing the altercations and verbal abuse in the home; and there the seeds for the cycle of children growing into adults who are either perpetrators or victims of abuse are planted and begin to grow.

What pictures are we painting for our children? It's never too late to grab a different brush and repaint your narrative.

Phoenix

Phoenix's story interested me greatly because of the sheer complexity of her thought process of how to be successful at relationships.

Her assessment of her mother and father, and the interactions between them, formed some deep, lasting impressions on her.

The conclusions she drew from how her father would act during conflict was very interesting. Her mother taking the stronger position whenever they had a disagreement and the subsequent divorce of her parents (initiated by her mother) allowed her to arrive at the conclusion that if you want your marriage or relationship to work, as a woman, you hide your strength. You don't exhibit or display assertiveness or confidence because it could cost you a marriage.

Being as close to her father as she was, it's not surprising that she felt that her father's attitude or behaviour was one she would rather emulate as opposed to her mother's.

Her father, in her eyes, was the victim, or the one who was misunderstood and needed to be cared for. Her mother being strong and assertive, and maybe domineering, repelled people and that wasn't what Phoenix wanted to do to loved ones.

What I also found really interesting was the importance that she placed on public opinion. It was really important to her that after having a child out of wedlock that she felt she had to acquire a certain status in life before she felt worthy of respect.

As I have mentioned before, too often women and girls are burdened with an image they are forced to fulfil before they are classed as worthy of so-called respect.

I have often said that if I wasn't married with children and had a weight problem, in certain societies, I would not be able to speak on the issues I raise without a barrage of abuse and disrespect. I have been accused of only working as an advocate for women and children because I'm single and can't have children – it would be funny if these people weren't serious.

Society does place a huge burden on us to fit into certain stereotypes or we aren't afforded the grace of an opinion, the right to set our boundaries or the audacity to live as we please and choose.

Phoenix felt the pressure of wanting to give the impression she had ticked the boxes and 'arrived', but ended up paying an exceptionally high price for the beautiful outward impression of a great marriage with her emotional, physical and mental health.

The other point of interest is the cultural element of how the domestic violence was addressed by the family.

Admittedly the family did well to give Phoenix the necessary support when they were first made aware of the problem, but notice that the extent of the family's contribution to resolving the issue was to tell the husband not to lay a finger on Phoenix again.

In this instance, it was sheer luck that such a brutal and violent man took heed, only for the type of abuse to change from physical abuse to more emotional and mental abuse; but abuse remained nonetheless.

Culture, tradition and religion all have the potential and capacity to act as enablers of domestic violence and indeed other types of abuse.

In many African cultures, it is frowned upon to encourage a woman to leave her matrimonial home, so much so that even where there has been physical abuse, the victim won't necessarily be encouraged or told outright to leave her husband.

Phoenix appears to have come from such a home, though compared to the norm, the family did expect answers for their daughter.

Phoenix chose to remain in the home because of the societal pressures that say you've failed if you divorce.

Her dumbing-down of herself to accept the abuse somehow told her that she would succeed in the long run, because she would succeed where her mother failed. Her emulating her father in her marriage further reinforced that notion.

The father's role is to build up and portray an image that is positive, and an atmosphere that's conducive to raising strong, confident and emotionally balanced children.

I believe what we're seeing here is a father-figure that may be perceived as weak or passive. As much as this image may not conjure up typical concerns, the effects on the girl child can be as detrimental as having a father that is domineering or abusive; only the manifestations by the child or adult female may be different.

The lack of strength in being unable to leave her husband can be attributed to the erosion of Phoenix's self-confidence and the constant put-downs from her husband, especially after the physical abuse stopped.

Many of us who work with victims of domestic violence especially, were overjoyed when the law in the UK was introduced to protect women from 'coercive control or controlling' domestic abuse – calling it now a criminal offence, carrying a sentence of up to five years.

Constantly calling your partner stupid, ugly, useless and fat and all the other insults these weak men throw at their wives and girlfriends, the constant humiliation, threat of violence to keep a woman or girl under control and the financial abuse that often comes with it, has found its way into the law books and has given another umbrella of hope to victims.

Now an abuser can no longer bask in the luxury of thinking action can only be taken where physical abuse has been committed. Greater measures are now in place to protect women, by taking a holistic view on how abuse happens, recognizing the different faces of domestic violence and seeking to protect women from all forms of it.

The definition of coercive behaviour has been described as: "Behaviour or an act or pattern of acts of assault, threats, humiliation and intimidation or other abuse that is used to harm, punish, or frighten their victim".

Coercive control can be used as a stepping stone to physically abuse one's partner, but now the law in the UK says it's not OK. Further provision in the law extends to close family members so it's encouraging to see that a well-rounded view of what really happens in abusive homes was taken into account when defining what coercive control means.

One thing I have realised, and this case is no different: many a time an emotionally or physically battered woman will leave her abusive partner not down to the worst beating she has received, but by something often unrelated to the typical abuse she's experiencing.

'The last straw that broke the camel's back'... a phrase I'm sure every woman in these circumstances has used may not be because of an attack.

It's ironic that Phoenix took on a persona of hiding her strength in her marriage thinking this is what would make it work, but to her children, it was strength they wanted to see in her by her being able to find the courage to leave... sometimes leaving, not staying, is where the ultimate power lies and is made manifest.

Chapter 16
A Mile In Your Shoes...

You see, life happens to the best of us, but we don't always recognise that others go through the same stuff we do because we only see what affects us; the world through our eyes and through our lenses only.

Life deals us different cards: to some we might feel we've been dealt a pack full of jokers, for others, a pack of aces.

For the majority of us, it's a mixture of both and depending on the game we're playing, we'll determine whether the hand we've been dealt will win or lose us the game.

It's always easy to relate to problems we've experienced or been exposed to, so in the absence of these two crucial elements, being able to place ourselves in the shoes of others can be challenging, sometimes even impossible.

The lack of exposure to certain life experiences also makes it hard to be empathetic to people who have suffered in areas where you hold strong opinions.

When you look at acts as heinous and as inhumane as domestic violence, rape and child abuse, one would assume that people would automatically sympathise with victims, but interestingly not everyone is moved by these things for an array of reasons.

People look at things from a very myopic angle that ultimately leads to victim-blaming.

Gender doesn't necessarily mean an automatic sympathetic ear. Sometimes we women can be the harshest critics of each other.

I recall reporting on a case on social media about a rape of a woman. A lady come onto the platform to say that the woman in question wouldn't have been raped if she had closed her legs tighter and had been serious enough in fending off her attacker... and no, I'm not kidding.

When I asked how she could possibly have come to this conclusion, her response was that no man could be strong enough to coordinate unzipping his trousers and prising open the legs of a fighting victim... yes... you read right. Your eyes are not deceiving you.

So shocked was I that I fortunately took screenshots of the exchange in case anyone thought this was too farfetched to be true.

So you see, other women can sometimes be the first to judge and condemn and express their indignation of how they would 'never let a man' rape, hit them or abuse them or their kids.

I recall another heated exchange after I discussed another rape case on one of my social media pages: A friend fiercely defended the attacker of the victim by not being convinced that they were genuinely raped because 'no woman would allow a man to rape her'. I don't think we've ever spoken again, after that conversation.

It doesn't make it too hard to see how rape victims are told in no uncertain terms to: be more careful, dress more appropriately, not to get drunk and if you're respectable, not to go into a man's or boy's room after a certain time if you have any self-respect and you're a 'nice girl'.

No mitigating circumstances are considered for the victim, only wilful and frighteningly subconscious support and understanding for the perpetrators of rape and abuse.

It's really no wonder why so many women and children remain tight-lipped about the abuse they suffer for fear of being judged, blamed and victimised all over again.

The parallel issues this raises is abusers are left to abuse freely, with not a single care in the world or worry of being held to account for their actions. Why? Because we have sorted out their alibis for them and the justifications for their actions.

Another interesting discussion I had about rape had a few men state that old chestnut about women's clothes being the reason for rape.

I had expressed my indignation and horror of a video of a well-known boxer in Africa fondling two young girls openly.

I was concerned about the boldness and seemingly acceptable manner of his actions as nobody seemed to raise any objections to the video circling on Facebook.

I raised issues around child sexual exploitation and the grooming process that children and young people are put through to be abused, and hoped to shed some light on this practice through that discussion.

These two 'gentlemen' were angry at the fact that I felt that the two young girls, who looked no more than about fifteen or sixteen at most, shouldn't be held to a higher account than this much older public figure.

Their argument was centred on their clothing and that if a young girl or woman dressed inappropriately, she had invariably made herself a candidate for rape and as such, if she was raped, it was her fault. The added fact that the girls weren't nine or ten meant that they knew what they were getting into so there was no real issue of abuse.

I asked the question to these two young men, to speak for themselves and not for the hypothetic actions of men they didn't know. What I was interested in was this, and this is what I asked them:

"Would YOU be willing to rape or sexually abuse another human being based on their attire because YOU felt their attire was inappropriate because if you wouldn't, please don't speak for anyone else. Speak for yourself. If you wouldn't rape someone based on their clothing, then that isn't a legitimate argument".

I'm still waiting for an answer from those two.

If we don't start to understand these issues, we will in no way be in a position to prevent rape, sexual abuse or domestic violence happening, or be in a position to educate anyone effectively on the subject.

We need an understanding of all the enablers and drivers of abuse and maybe, just maybe, we'll be able to be aware of the signs we can look out for to try and put a stop to it.

People sometimes feel that OK, rape and sexual abuse can be argued that there are mitigating circumstances as to why there are victims, but domestic violence surely is something 'they' didn't need to tolerate, because they could leave if they could just be bothered to pack a case and stay with friends.

Really?...

There are many different reasons why a woman may find herself in an abusive relationship and it would be my hope and wish that this far down the line, that it was understandable and fathomable how victims of abuse are created.

It's a frightening level of ignorance that would blame anyone who, through inexperience, naivety or gullibility, found themselves in the situations that we've read about from four very brave women.

Even in situations where there is a repeat of circumstances and behaviour, it's a lot more complicated than people just learning their lesson and doing better next time. As I said: the more we judge, the more we drive victims underground and the more we create environments for self-blame and free reign for abusers.

Telling victims to just get up and leave or asking why they put up with the behaviour really isn't helpful, as if they don't know that the situations or relationships they are in are bad for them.

Those questions and disapproving comments do nothing to equip and empower an abuse victim to leave her abuser. It will serve us well to understand that abusers start with the mind before it progresses to the fist for victims of domestic violence.

In all our getting, let's get understanding.

I would hope that from what has been demonstrated, we've acquired some amount of knowledge to appreciate that it takes more than just a little willpower to make that move from victim to victor.

Aside from physical shifts to move out of a toxic relationship, the real shift needs to be a mental and emotional shift.

To be totally honest, it's the mind that needs the most work; moving your physical location is the 'easy' bit.

On the flip side, I have also heard many times people giving advice to women in toxic and abusive relationships to stay put, especially where children are involved.

I have heard a vast number of reasons but one that often pops up is the fact that the woman made the poor choice to get involved with the man in the first place, and therefore it's her lot and she should just stay; this has always bothered me.

There are a number of drivers to this kind of thinking and advice. Reasons ranging from religious beliefs to family values; all seem to act as a voice that assumes the right to determine the standard of what is considered as appropriate behavior for a woman when it comes to leaving her marital home.

By no means, as I've mentioned before, is the imposition appropriate for making the woman the sole person responsible for maintaining her home.

The other reason I often come across is because it's somehow seen as a disgrace to have children from different men, some women are encouraged to have all their children from the same man, irrespective of whether that man is abusive or not. So long as the woman can tick a box to say that all kids belong to the same father, that's all that matters.

I have always found this particular piece of advice exceptionally reckless and quite offensive.

It offends me because I feel at the point at which a victim is disclosing that they're being abused, unless they're already pregnant, is that the time to still reinforce the cultural status quo at all costs? Is that really the priority at a time like that?

It's really sad that we are forced or encouraged to continue to have children for a man that is abusive and is probably not a great father to the children he already has anyway; why up the quota for there to be more casualties of a domestic war?

Domestic violence is really hard on children.

The mental pressure on such children is profound and devastating. Seeing your mother being beaten and hurt is too much for children to have to deal with.

Feelings of anxiety, despair, being forced to keep the secret of the home, just pile on the pressure on these children mentally. The children often walk on tenterhooks as a result of the unpredictability of the attacks; after all, they won't always know what the trigger will be for their father or mother's partner to set off the next beating or verbal assault, sometimes not just exclusive to the mother.

A child's need to want to protect their mother and them being unable to do so, no matter what age they are, can leave them feeling helpless, vulnerable and useless.

It's amazing how little we realise how depression in children becomes commonplace when raised in a violent home for all the above reasons.

Affection, reassurance and stability is woefully lacking in an abusive home and children are left pretty much to their own devices to find their way during and after the violent episodes in the home. This isn't to say the mothers aren't affectionate and loving; far from it! But during episodes of violence, at a time when children will need the most reassurance, the mother will not be in a position to give it.

We have a good idea of what women in physically abusive homes go through, as we've had some very graphic pictures presented to us. From some of the stories we've read, we should realise that to encourage a woman to have more children in a relationship that is abusive is as irresponsible as it is wicked.

Chapter 17
Happily Ever After...

As a Christian, I have heard many times how badly God views divorce and as a such, no excuse is really acceptable to take this course of action, regardless of abuse being the reason for the divorce.

Being a woman of the church and having lived on planet Earth long enough to appreciate some of the challenges that we face, I think I'm in a good enough position to share my take on this issue from a biblical perspective.

I once heard a message that spoke of the failure of both men and women in the church if they divorced and not to see the breakdown of their marriage as some sort of achievement; it's to be seen as a failure and nothing else.

I strongly disagree.

I love my pack or cards and I want to bring them out again: Your pack of cards may be very different to mine, and if I try and play my hand with the set that you've been dealt and not mine, I think it's safe to say there might be a bit of a problem.

For all we know, we might not even be playing the same card game.

Marriage is as unique as the people within it, as are the challenges and problems they face.

When a woman is living with abuse within a marriage, it's a very hard place to be.

When tradition, culture, religion, family and other similar elements are thrown in, it raises additional hurdles for the abused woman to consider and jump through in order to set herself free.

Very few women are able to walk out of an abusive marriage without support from the places where they mostly expect it, and unfortunately the areas I've mentioned don't always come through for her.

Too often women are told to suck it up and lie on the bed they've made, but is this right? Is this fair?

When it comes to the church, we don't often have enough understanding and compassion to understand how hellish living with an abusive partner can actually be.

We need to be clear on what the Bible actually says about marriage and what constitutes a good home.

My intention is not to preach here, but I know from experience there are women in the church struggling with leaving an abusive partner due to the misinterpretation of what marriage is supposed to be, and the misinterpretation of the role the husband is supposed to play in the home.

The following extract is from chapter 5:21-33 in the book of Ephesians; this is what it says in the Amplified version:

Instructions for Christian Households

21 Submit to one another out of reverence for Christ.

22 Wives, submit yourselves to your own husbands as you do to the Lord. 23 For the husband is the head of the wife as Christ is the head of the church, his body, of which he is the Saviour. 24 Now as the church submits to Christ, so also wives should submit to their husbands in everything.

25 Husbands, love your wives, just as Christ loved the church and gave himself up for her 26 to make her holy, cleansing[b] her by the washing with water through the word, 27 and to present her to himself as a radiant church, without stain or wrinkle or any other blemish, but holy and blameless. 28 In this same way, husbands ought to love their wives as their own bodies. He who loves his wife loves himself. [29] After all, no one ever hated their own body, but they feed and care for their body, just as Christ does the church— [30] for we are members of his body. [31] "For this reason a man will leave his father and mother and be united to his wife, and the two will become one flesh."[c] [32] This is a profound mystery—but I am talking about Christ and the church. [33] However, each one of you also must love his wife as he loves himself, and the wife must respect her husband.

Firstly this chapter talks of both parties submitting to one another; neither party is more important nor of greater value than the other.

In this current age of equality, the issue of women submitting to men fills most females with horror and indignation at the thought of anyone being the head of them.

This passage has been interpreted to mean that women should be subservient to men and should be good little ladies and do what they're told, no matter what the situation dictates or what is being meted out to them – abuse, rape and violence being no exceptions.

In the context of what the Bible is speaking about, this is very much a convenient misinterpretation when relayed to mean that wives or women should submit to men at all times, at all costs, come what may... NO!

Interestingly, from verse 25, the passage gives meticulous instruction on the role of the husband in the marriage.

Husbands are not just told to love their wives in a way that they must figure out for themselves, but they are deliberately and purposefully told how.

According to the Bible, Christ gave His life for the church, i.e. for mankind. His sacrificing His life was demonstrative and indicative of the height, breadth and depth of love He felt for the world.

This passage is unambiguous in the picture it paints and the message it gives in directing husbands to love their wives in this way; nothing more and nothing less. The instruction is to love with everything that they have until it costs them their life if it has to, and that is not in a murder-suicide context!

The further elaboration on how no man would hate his own body was an additional dimension to the picture of how healthy love and marriage looks. The instruction therefore for women to submit to husbands, contrary to what has been peddled as oppression, was merely to instruct that the ultimate responsibility of the home was for the husband to lead through love and respect and to submit to it. After all, if this love was guarded by his life you can expect him to want to know that the wife is totally worth it – not a bad deal.

Now, whether you agree with this passage in the Bible and what it says or not is irrelevant in the context of the point being made here.

For the Christian woman, this is the framework in which she is asked to operate. The point of debate and discussion should rest around the man a woman is being convinced not to leave, who is abusive, has clearly not lived up to this standard, and therefore should the wife not be able to renegotiate her position in the marriage contract?

In any contract, the other party is relieved of their obligations to fulfil their contractual responsibilities if the other party has rescinded on theirs.

Too often the issue of submission is used to gag women in the church from divorcing.

When a woman presents an issue in her home, the usual focus is on the wife and it being her job, for making the marriage work being placed solely on her, regardless of what the issue is. At best the husband will get a slap on the wrist followed by all eyes and attention on the Mrs. to put things right thereafter.

Another interesting verse that's used is, 'God hates divorce'...

That's great but that's not the whole verse, just the first few words.

The full passage makes reference to God's feelings about domestic violence. This is what it says:

Malachi 2:16 Amplified Bible (AMP)

[16] *"For I hate divorce," says the LORD, the God of Israel, "and him who covers his garment with wrong and violence," says the LORD of hosts. "Therefore keep watch on your spirit, so that you do not deal treacherously [with your wife]."*

The above speaks partly of violence within marriage.

The wife is referred to as the garment of the husband.

One would be hard pressed to find any scriptures that supports the subjugation of women and the maltreatment of such, so it's very sad to witness time and time again the support of ill treatment of women in some churches and the Bible used as a basis for this!

In an ideal world we should understand that a sense of responsibility towards anyone who is vulnerable in our society benefits that same society.

There needs to be more visible, tangible emotional and psychological support for women who disclose that they are suffering abuse. There should be more support offered by the church to deal with such matters so that they don't act as enablers for abuse to be carried out, uninterrupted and unchallenged.

Church is supposed to be a haven; a spiritual hospital for the sick to recover. Nobody goes in perfect and nobody comes out perfect, but there's a hope that all patients will get the medicine they need.

By no means do I mean to imply that these attitudes are only found in the Christian religion.

I have counselled and coached many women from various religious backgrounds: Jewish, Moslem and Hindu women and many others have crossed my path. If it's not the religious practices that are keeping some of these women bound, it's the cultural or traditional practices doing the same job.

Am I anti-religion or anti-marriage? Not at all! I've already failed on both counts if I were. I am however anti-hiding behind religion, culture and tradition to turn a blind eye to the suffering of women and children; I am anti-silence in these areas being used to mute, deny and be passive to women that need help and support to save their lives and sanity and that of their children.

Our beliefs are there to act as a moral compass to give us direction and a standard at which to operate to be decent and compassionate people, not perfect people.

We're all suffering from different 'ailments' and we should never be in a place that puts anyone in a position to suffer more than they need to.

I hope that if any woman is suffering abuse, being manipulated into staying in an abusive home or being asked to cover up abuse, they should know that if they believe in God, God is love and doesn't advocate abuse of any kind.

If any pastors, fathers, vicars, imams, rabbis or whoever, use religion as a basis to coerce you to stay, do so by your own volition but do not stay to please God, because you're no use to God broken, battered, bruised or dead.

Compassion is a wonderful thing that needs to work for those who have had to deal with the level of adversity that they have experienced or are experiencing, and this compassion should be even more visible within our religious practices and places of worship especially.

Compassion simply says, 'I don't profess to understand it, but I'm here for you to help you get through it.'

When we can all come to that place, we make it safe for victims of abuse to transition to being survivors of abuse.

Chapter 18
Getting Out The Kitchen...

The realisation that your relationship is failing or has failed is a tough realisation to face up to, and rarely thought about in isolation from all the other things that are associated with that revelation.

We go into a relationship hoping for its success but when this doesn't happen and you come to accept that you have to leave, what do you do?

Having had an interesting discussion with three women on the subject of marriage and emotional abuse, I was asked: 'So what do you do when you realise all these things (realising you want to leave after accepting what you've gone through has been abusive) and you have kids? It's not easy to leave. Sometimes don't you just have to stay and deal with it?'

I guess there's no easy answer to this question if you want an honest response to it.

I mentioned before that real lasting change has to start with self and that is a mental shifting in how you see yourself, the situation you're in, what you want to do about it and where you see yourself being in the future.

When you come to the realisation that you have reached a point within you that you can no longer continue in your relationship or marriage under circumstances that no longer suits you, you will invariably cause a major shift in your partnership once you begin to operate from that place.

There's no blanket answer to the question I was asked.

Would you leave an abusive relationship just because I or anyone else asked you to do so? I think not.

That move is only made when you decide to move; very little can be done to force even the most violently abused woman to move until she is ready to do so. Her reasons to remain are complex and multifaceted, hence why I mentioned a mental relocation being more permanent than a physical move from an abusive relationship to a safe house.

One cannot claim to understand all the factors that contribute to an abused woman being in the relationship she's in (in the absence of thorough psychological analysis) any more than one can provide a solution.

The change that happens internally, that makes you decide that you cannot continue to suffer in the relationship any longer, can cause a restlessness in your spirit because your mind tells you that remaining mentally or physically stationary is no longer an option.

The abusive partner of a woman in this state may continue to deliver their abuse unaltered, but their abuse is unlikely to be received in the same way by the victim because of the mental shift of the victim. The dynamics of that union would have to change even though the abuser may be oblivious to this change initially.

The manifestation of this change may not be outward to begin with, but even the mental shift means the hold of the abuser will have to slacken; this is especially the case for emotional or psychological abusers.

The power of the abuser is in the subject accepting the abuse and acting in line as a victim; the change in perception of self in deciding that enough is enough. This is sufficient to start tipping the scales to balance out the scales of power and eventually tip it in favour of the woman who has now found her voice and right to demand not to be a victim any longer.

There are real challenges that women face when the decision is made to move on.

Money can be one of those issues and can be a big reason to remain in an abusive home. Again, it's not for anyone to judge what this looks like because different people have different fears for themselves and their children not being able to eat or have a roof over their heads.

Not everyone is fortunate enough to live in a country that makes provision for women who are facing abuse. Even in the United Kingdom, the system is far from perfect. Cuts to charitable organisations have crippled many charities from being able to provide the services so desperately required for women fleeing domestic violence in the manner that they are used to.

Some women feel that it's the price they are obliged to pay for the education of their children and to keep them fed and watered.

The mental trauma and mental health of children living with domestic violence and other abuse is a luxury some women feel they can't afford to dwell on, when the visible physical needs of their child are what they see; however I am absolutely not talking about a mother allowing her child to suffer so she can enjoy luxuries in life, as we have heard from Malia's story.

More often than not, there is financial abuse along with the physical violence so money isn't always at the disposal of the victim, even when the victim is working, because the abusive partner may insist on taking the earnings of the victim to reinforce their agenda of isolation and complete dependency on them.

I did say this wasn't an easy question to answer.

I can only stress that change will need to happen and when it does, the answers to the how? when? and what? will come in time; the first step in answering those questions is to make the decision to take back the control first.

It's important to mention that the answers required will be unique and right for the woman asking them. The solution for a victim of abuse cannot ever be a one size fits all, even if the presented issues may look identical on the surface.

The level of intervention to put a mother and her family or a woman on her own, back to an emotional equilibrium, will always be tailored to that particular woman and set of circumstances, because you're dealing with unique and special individuals.

I have mentioned the challenges around women in some churches being placed under pressure to remain in unhealthy marriages, and we know there are other factors that contribute to forcing women to stay put.

In many cultures and certain social classes, it's frowned upon to be divorced. Somehow the men never seem to be looked down on and the women rarely seem to be given the same advice that their male counterparts are given about divorce.

We are automatically the losers, the failures, the non-respectable individuals that will dare to let their marriage fail.

Doesn't matter if the man was unfaithful, doesn't matter if he's beating you, doesn't matter if he's interfering with the kids, just don't get divorced and bring shame on the family!

Only you can decide if this is reason enough to stay.

That mental assessment of who you are and what makes you feel ashamed is yours alone to determine and define.

I recall being in a relationship once where I was terribly unhappy.

One day something just popped in my head and I remember thinking, 'There's nobody here. Just me. Nobody can see if I'm happy or sad, just me. I'm here trying to be a picture of something I'm not and I'm the only one suffering; this is foolish. Everyone else is living their life and this is mine.'

I started to put plans in motion to leave.

Perception of me to others in that defining moment was irrelevant to my life. I just couldn't continue to pretend to the world that I was happy whilst I was dying on the inside.

So what am I saying? Only you can know when it's the right time to leave an unhappy or abusive relationship or marriage.

Only you can put into action the mechanisms required to take back your life.

Yes, of course it's hard when you have children, and we often use the children as a reason or excuse to stay.

'The kids are too close to their dad' and 'the children need their father' are very common reasons and excuses. I use the words 'excuses' and 'reasons' because sometimes they're both.

Remember our pictures of what we are allowing our children to see through what we introduce into the home? You have to decide if you're able to take the responsibility of what your children are witnessing and how that will impact them in future.

This walk is too personal for anyone to instruct you to do anything, but when you're ready to make a decision to do something, then there is help out there to support you to make that move.

Trusting the right person or authorities to confide in or seek help from when we're going through an abusive relationship is always a huge challenge.

We feel ashamed, guilty, stupid and an array of other things which help to further silence and isolate us from reaching out or having anyone reach out to us.

The funny thing is, there are so many women who have gone through what you may be experiencing, and if you are able to connect with women who have been through these similar issues and who have come out the other side, then know that there's hope - know that you really aren't alone.

There are very few problems in this world that haven't been witness or experienced.

Where abuse has taken place, it is totally understandable that trust needs to be built after having trust betrayed, but you can start gathering your building blocks to start building trust again; what you've been through doesn't have to be the end of your story.

Chapter 19
Forgiveness...

When we're hurt or let down, there is usually one of two sources responsible for that emotion: either we have let ourselves down or someone else has done the honours, and maybe there's a third being a combination of the two.

Different people handle offence, or whatever you wish to call it, in a way that's familiar to them and in line with their personality and experience of how they behave when they have been let down.

Our emotions are there for a reason, and it's never healthy to shut them off, because how we feel helps us to understand the appropriate reactions and responses to give or not give to the situations that have brought about those emotions.

When we are dictated to in how we should feel, it can lead to an immense amount of frustration and can be very damaging to our emotional independence, and interferes with our emotional authority and ability to heal.

Various cultures deal with offence differently and I have had the pleasure of seeing these differing reactions in a few cultures.

Take the British, for example, and I generalise here: never wanting to make a fuss and complain – even if they are offended.

The 'stiff upper lip' saying wasn't created out of nowhere. You suck it up and just get on with it, but do you?

Your upper lip can be as stiff as it likes, but it won't stop the bottom lip from quivering or the tears from stinging your eyes.

The Americans are generally very vocal and won't usually hesitate to tell you how they feel; I witnessed this quite a lot during my frequent visits to the States when I used to sing, especially with the New Yorkers.

Then there's Africa; it's a big place so I'll narrow it down to the one place I know well, and that's Ghana.

A very placid group of people, who have a 'Give it to God' attitude because Ghanaians are very religious. Doesn't really matter what has happened, you're supposed to just let things go so everyone can move on quickly as if nothing happened – even though it has.

Long drawn out discussions on emotional conflict just aren't encouraged.

I could go all around the world but just a general overview of how diverse our dealings with offence and hurt are, based on our backgrounds, is quite interesting to observe. It can explain quite a lot about how or why we handle certain situations in the manner that we do, and how certain groups might cope with emotional issues as opposed to others.

In some parts of the world and amongst certain people, not a lot of emphasis is placed on emotional or mental wellbeing, so little investment is made in or is available for practices such as counselling and other therapies, as a result of the culture in those places.

Contrary to just stereotyping groups of people, it's actually quite important to be aware of the level of influence culture, tradition and even religion have to play in something so common but yet so complex amongst the different groups of people we encounter.

If we gain this type of intelligence, it will help us to be more aware and therefore better able to be supportive of people that need a sounding board or need help to deal with their problems and just as importantly, to know the style and manner in which we will offer that help and support.

Understanding forgiveness and offence is particularly important in being able to support yourself through the healing process as well as obtaining this knowledge to help others.

Forgiveness is a journey. It's a journey the hurt or offended party must embark on alone and at their own pace. Of course a supportive hand won't do any harm, but ultimately, the offended party is the only one that has the luxury of forgiving the person or persons who have hurt them.

If you have caused offence, forgiveness is the one thing you cannot demand as a right - you can only request it or at most, beg for it.

When someone has gone through something such as sexual abuse, rape, domestic violence or a deep betrayal, nobody really has the right or privilege to dictate how that individual is to respond to that offence or to demand that they forgive the offender. They neither have the right to set the timeframe for when that forgiveness is manifested, nor the form in which the forgiveness should take.

The reasons I have seen for this happening are to tell the offended or aggrieved party that they can't fully heal unless they've forgiven the person who has hurt them; but is this right?

If our concern is really the healing and emotional and psychological restoration of the person concerned, why would you not first find out what they need to feel emotionally liberated?

We have read stories of women who have been through profound life experiences which, to this point, have had an adverse and monumental effect on their lives.

It's immensely insensitive and totally inappropriate to demand that they act in a particular way, usually to make the person making that demand feel more comfortable about the situation the abused person is struggling with, as opposed to really seeing the person restored.

Usually the refusal to be involved with the person who has committed the offence is interpreted as the offended person having not really forgiven.

Let me explain something many people get really mixed up and confused about: relationship and forgiveness are two different things and I'll explain why.

Some relationships are quite simply toxic in their nature.

A relationship, for example, that doesn't allow you to be yourself, leaves you feeling bad about who you are, doesn't allow you to mature or better yourself, where your needs are ignored or never met – you get the picture? This is a toxic relationship and when you realise it and decide to extricate yourself from it, you shouldn't feel guilty for having done so.

You may come to a place where you have been able to work through the issues that this relationship posed to you and you're ready to move on; forgiveness does not, and I repeat, does not mean you having to maintain a relationship with this person. Let us not forget: it is our choice who we allow to be in our emotional space.

If you have figured out the pattern of behaviour on your part that allows you to be treated in a manner that is unhealthy for you, then it's your right to decide not to carry on a relationship that enables them to continue their attitude in a way that no longer serves you.

If you do decide to keep the relationship, then you also have the right to set boundaries, the prerogative to put down the necessary demarcations for you to function from a good and sound place.

In all honesty, in any relationship it's necessary to set boundaries. People know where they stand and they're able to manage their interactions with you knowing what is acceptable and what is not.

I remember watching a programme on TV where the young lady had slept with her best friend's boyfriend. The crowd were all vying for the friends to make up and they did... I watched with interest and amusement as these two young ladies turned on the rat of a boyfriend, claiming that they were best friends after all and that nobody, especially boyfriends, should come between them.

It's the best friend's choice to forgive her friend, but if she wants to manage the relationship and minimise there being a repeat of the situation, she might want to draw some boundaries.

Let me give an analogy for the purpose of clarity:

Imagine you're a friend of mine and I find out you've stolen money from me; I'm naturally upset and you apologise for the theft.

We make up and I invite you over for dinner. My handbag is beside me when I decide I need the ladies' room. What should I do with my bag? Should I leave it there because we're friends as I've forgiven you, or would it be wise, as a precaution, to take my bag with me?

Relationships where trust has been broken look something like that; forgiveness is one thing, trust is another.

Forgiveness, as with relationships, is not synonymous with trust; they are actually three very separate entities altogether.

As I said earlier, different people need different things before they can forgive someone that's done something to them that's made them feel horrible.

Some people need to have a certain type of closure before they're able to move on and this is why it's unhelpful to ignore someone's healing process or to hamper it by a one-size-fits-all approach.

The idea of confronting someone who has hurt us can be daunting for some but for others, this is what they need to be able to move on and set themselves free from whatever has held them emotionally bound.

Confronting someone who has wronged you should be dealt with with caution, by ensuring that you manage your expectations before you embark on that mission.

I recall a close friend of mine, who had a particularly difficult relationship with their parents, came to me to say they wanted to confront them about things they felt had affected them adversely in their adult life because of their childhood.

I thought that it might be helpful to offer them some perspective on what they wanted to do so I asked what they expected from them.

There was a long pause, then a very defensive explanation of what had been done to them and the cost to their happiness later on in life.

I repeated the question about expectation because they hadn't actually given me an answer, so I elaborated:

'There are in my mind a few options about managing your expectations when confronting someone who you feel has wronged you.

'If you don't decide what they are or what you want, you could end up more wounded after you see them than you are now, so it's really important that you manage your expectations from the outset, with a clear goal in mind for this conversation that you want to have.

'Here are your options:

If you want an apology and are hoping they'll offer one with no prompting from you and you don't get one, what will you do if you don't get it? How would that look or feel to you and where does that leave you?

If you have to ask for or demand an apology and it's given, but not sincere, what do you do?

If they refuse to apologise, where does that leave you in your healing process?

Do you just need to offload and be heard, apologies not being the most important part of this process?

If so, say what you want and leave the rest for them to decide what they wish to do with the information you've given.'

I received an even longer pause than the one I had before I presented these options. My friend was very reflective and said, 'You're right. If I went there and they were dismissive of me, that would really hurt me.'

I had gathered that to have been the case when I asked the question and was pleased that they had considered their options as a result of it.

They felt far more in control and empowered by having a set objective in their mind, so that their whole approach in speaking to their parents was far more coherent, structured and practical than it would have been.

My friend opted to just be heard and leave it at that; I felt this was a good choice.

I have observed that when we tie our healing journey to the acknowledgement or appreciation of our pain to another human being, we disempower ourselves greatly.

If our ability to move on is in any way dependent on the apology of another, then we may have a very long wait.

Sometimes the truth of the matter is that the person who has hurt us just doesn't care. They don't care about what they've said or done to hurt you, and they may never have that epiphany. Where does that leave you?

Don't cause yourself more distress over something you cannot possibly control. The only thing you can control is you, remember?

The best place to be is where you offload your troubles and walk away. The one thing that person cannot be is oblivious to your suffering but if you can, leave it there. Don't hide around the corner to see what they do with your box of pain. You've dropped it off, leave it! It's not your problem. What they do with it is their business, not yours – you've got a life to live.

Some people just aren't wired to feel remorse, or compassion, or mercy, and probably take some pleasure in knowing that they hold that trump card of apology over your life because they sense you're waiting for them to acknowledge your pain before you can move on.

Take your power back. Grab that card out of their hand and play your own aces.

One of the greatest and possibly most difficult things to do is not to forgive a person who has hurt you, but rather to forgive yourself.

It's one of the single most liberating, uplifting and kindest things you can do for yourself, but the journey in being able to get there is tough, really tough.

There are so many things that we go through that we wouldn't have done if we had had the benefit of hindsight.

I love the saying 'youth is wasted on the young', because it really does epitomise the situation many of us find ourselves in when we've made mistakes and regretted them.

Nobody knows the future and sometimes our lack of experience, youth, and the following of bad or poor advice or none at all, can mean we make decisions based on the absolute nothingness that we have to draw from.

Sometimes we think we know what we're doing, only to realise that we have in fact made a wrong turn or wrong decision and we're left to put back the pieces of what we've done, but often the damage has already been done and what has gone wrong just can't be fixed… and that's the beginning of the end for some of us.

Regret can be one of the most time destructive feelings we can allow ourselves to experience.

We can't change the past; no matter how hard we try, we just cannot go back in time and undo what was done, whether we did whatever it was to ourselves or something was done to us.

What we do have the power to change is the here and now.

I think it's essential that we all explore and question things from our past if there are areas that need fixing. I believe it to be of great benefit if we go back to 'gather intelligence' for the purposes of knowing what information we need to make a difference in our lives today in terms of balance and wellbeing for our emotions and mental health.

When we regret things to the point of blaming ourselves, we harbour unforgiving feelings that can be very damaging. It's as if we need to stay in that place to feel the pain and punish ourselves for our failings or shortcomings.

In not forgiving ourselves for things that we have done wrong, we deny ourselves permission to let 'it' go and live life without the baggage of regret and punishment.

We stay stagnant and in limbo, making whatever it was have total power over our most precious possession – and that's time.

Time either improves the situation or makes it worse.

Living and wallowing in regret in what could have been, but wasn't, serves very little purpose in adding value to our lives and affecting our current state for the better.

You have the right to be happy. That's the simple truth, regardless of what has happened to you or you did to yourself.

It's OK to learn to love yourself, even with the mistakes you've made.

At some point, a decision has to be made to resolve to acknowledge and take note of where you went wrong, accept your mistakes, look at what you can and will do differently and MOVE ON!

You have the absolute right to experience real joy and not be judged on your mistakes of the past or to pay for them for the rest of your life.

If you're truly sorry, you can truly be forgiven; permission to enjoy the one life and live it to the full, has been granted.

Chapter 20
Restoration, Healing &
Hope For The Future...

Nobody asks to be born into an abusive home or asks to be in a dangerous or emotionally volatile and unstable relationship.

Childhood traumas, especially those around emotional, sexual, physical and mental abuse, create a solid foundation to derail a person to fail at life, avoiding all the good things that they should have been able to enjoy and set them up emotionally and mentally to live life to the full.

We have looked at the various ways restoration can happen for us from counselling, transformational life coaching, psychotherapy, psychiatry and cognitive behavioural therapy to other forms of therapy that can give balance and put someone who has suffered childhood trauma in a restorative state.

There are so many effects of abuse in childhood or as young people that have a direct impact on the adult we become.

For example: untreated childhood trauma can contribute to drug and alcohol dependency in later life. This is usually with the intention of blocking out the pain of what has been experienced.

More often than not, being in a state of inebriation or being under the influence of drugs has the effect of delaying the healing process because pain is being numbed and not allowed to surface to be confronted and dealt with.

It takes a hell of a lot to allow yourself to be emotionally exposed to things you would rather were hidden. I purposely haven't said forgotten, because nobody really forgets. Trauma can cause your mind to bury painful and frightening memories but in God's infinite wisdom, the trauma of what is suffered is always stored somewhere in the brain.

With the skills and areas of holistic and conventional medical practices, those memories can possibly be brought to the surface so they can be addressed and filed away safely, as opposed to being buried out of fear.

Much of my work involves helping my clients to get to a place where they feel safe and ready to speak about what, to them, was once unspeakable.

Creating a space for an individual to feel able to release the words they have never spoken to anyone is a powerful thing for that person, and is the beginning of restoration and them putting the measures in place to get their life back.

Not enough support is given to children who have suffered trauma. Help often takes too long to be implemented and if it does, it's not always for long enough to be the outlet and safe place that's needed to get out all that's required to set the scales in balance.

It's normally pretty easy to predict that a child who has suffered abuse will need emotional support but with adults, this can be very different.

Because adults can decide what we want to do, we can't enforce or insist on therapy for them, neither can we decide what is in their best interest if they have the mental capacity to make decisions for themselves. If a person doesn't ask for emotional or psychological help as quickly as we would like them to, then their healing and restoration can be hampered and delayed.

It never ceases to amaze me how in this day and age, some people still have quite negative preconceived ideas about the value and the importance of counselling, psychotherapy and other interventions that deal with the health of the mind.

We're quite happy to see a doctor for physical ailments but immediately it's not to do with the body, we suddenly feel different rules apply, as if we somehow qualify for an award for figuring everything out ourselves that is non-physical.

There should be absolutely no shame in seeking help to empower us to heal our emotions and our minds.

Mental health issues can stem not just from the trauma that has been suffered by a victim, but the lack of intervention when that trauma was realised.

It's not uncommon for children, and indeed adults, depending on what type of trauma they've experienced, to feel that whatever they were going through was normal. It's not always obvious that abuse was wrong, as crazy as that may sound to some of you.

To come to a place and a realisation that what happened was not normal or OK is a hurdle and a difficulty in itself; to jump that hurdle successfully can mean you need help in being able doing so.

If early intervention happens when abuse or trauma has occurred, the risk of drug and alcohol dependency, other addictions, mental and general health problems can be minimized or avoided..

I have become a great advocate for hypnotherapy used as a tool to deal with the effects of trauma, due to its effectiveness in dealing with traumas that particularly may have been hidden from the conscious mind.

I've touched on this previously, about trauma being concealed, and I would like to elaborate a little more here.

The revelation of a deeply devastating encounter in someone's childhood only coming to light in adulthood can be very destabilising, but at the same time can be the key they've been searching for to make sense of why things have happened in their life in the manner that it did.

Suffering from mental illness, anxiety, self-harm and other evidence of something that the mind is struggling to cope with, and that is showing up in our life in various ways, can sometimes be as a result of something deeply wrong that our conscious mind can't recall.

The cognitive and emotional status of children isn't one where anybody can expect them to handle traumatic situations and events beyond their years. To a degree they lack the tools to rationalise what they have gone through, somethings that even adults struggle with.

Locking those memories away is not unusual. It's not strange for the mind to have the ability to archive harmful memories so the rest of the body, mind and soul can function as best it can.

Unlocking them is where hypnotherapy, especially in the areas of energetic somatic release, containment and corrective experience, is used to bring healing by dealing with those harmful feeling and memories.

Other behavioural manifestations such as anxiety and anger can be something that a person who has suffered trauma experiences, but has no idea that it may be attributed to a negative event in the past.

I have spoken to people who have suffered with addiction and who have tried to kick whatever habit they have had, without realising that the source of the issue they really needed to deal with was the trauma.

The addiction essentially can be a byproduct of something else that has gone on; a symptom and definitely not always the cause of the addiction.

These revelations aren't always easy to discover independent of help, and this is why it's so important to consider what assistance is out there and to determine what is right for you.

I had a client who had been raped and didn't want to go for counselling because she wasn't happy with an experience she had had following the attack. She felt she was being judged by the counsellor because of some of the things she shared during the few sessions she had with the counsellor.

She expressed her desire to work with me, based purely on trust and the fact that she knew I would always hold her in a positive non-judgemental space; she essentially trusted me as a person as well as a professional.

One of the key issues here is finding someone to work with

that you absolutely trust, have a rapport with and feel you can be totally open with.

Find someone to work and walk with you on your healing journey that will always hold you in unconditional positive regard, irrespective of what you present to them.

This will go a long way in allowing you to be completely transparent and will help you to delve into areas within yourself without fear of judgement or prejudice; without it, your healing and liberation may be greatly hampered with the person you've chosen to work with you. There must be absolute respect between you and your chosen professional, regardless of the category of interventionist they fall under.

I cannot stress enough how important it is that you have an open mind in what it might take for you to find the right fit.

Please don't do yourself the injustice of writing off counsellors because of a bad experience, or a psychologist because of something they said.

Nobody in any profession speaks for everyone. Interview the person you wish to employ to help you do one of the most important things you'll ever do in your life, and that is to attain and master emotional and mental freedom to live the best version of your life that you can possibly live.

Life really is too short! Very cliché I know, but the clichés are usually the best because they turn out to be true.

You only get one shot at this. So you mess up or someone messes you up somewhere along the line, and so what?

You're not the first and unfortunately you won't be the last, so do yourself the favour of deciding not to continue to beat yourself up for the experiences you've had. Cut yourself a break; the only thing you need to do is make a choice and that is to start to build or rebuild your life.

The most important part of your journey is realisation and revelation. If you've been able to identify any patterns in yourself then you have a chance to make a change.

Change will wait for you, but the terms and conditions may alter. Go for it while it has its special offers and grab it now.

Don't give up on a chance to be healed and happy. I know you might have tried before and failed, but please don't give up. There are so many of us here waiting just to hold your hand and tell you that it'll be OK, that you are not to blame for the things you've gone through and that nobody is judging you.

Healing is a right. Happiness is a right. Peace is a right. Loving yourself is a right. The only privilege is choosing people like me to be humbled by being given the chance to help you.

Now go ahead and be the best you, you can be.

Written by Dilys Sillah